Comeback

One Man's Triumph
Over a Near Death Experience

Comeback

One Man's Triumph
Over a Near Death Experience

by
Douglas Sandoval

Light
of
Hope
Press

Comeback: One Man's Triumph Over a Near Death Experience

Printed in the United States

Published by
Light of Hope Press
Los Angeles, California 90043
douglas4107@gmail.com
www.comebackdouglas.com

Edited by Yvonne Hutchinson
Designed by Alan Bell

Publisher's Cataloging-In-Publication Data
(Prepared by The Donohue Group, Inc.)
Names: Sandoval, Douglas.
Title: Comeback: one man's triumph over a near death experience / by Douglas Sandoval.
Description: [Los Angeles, California] : [Light of Hope Press], [2018] | Identifiers: ISBN 9781532388941

Library of Congress Control Number:
Light of Hope Press, Los Angeles, California

Table of Contents

For with God nothing shall be impossible.

Luke 1:37

Comeback

One Man's Triumph
Over a Near Death Experience

Acknowledgements

First, I want to thank My Lord God for giving a second chance at life and for bringing some wonderful people into my life after this horrific incident.

I would like to thank my mom, Sofia Sandoval, for being there for me all these years and especially these last 15 years. She has been so patient with me all those months and all those long years of therapy and "for your sleepless nights." Mom: You are my number one inspiration.

I want to thank my kids, Diana, Joshua, Douglas Jr, Alex, Hellen, Matthew and Janet. I want you guys to know that you were my inspiration through all those years along with Mom.

I want to be sure to thank my wonderful wife, Victoria Acosta, for your support and your prayers.

Thanks to the doctors and nurses from Harborview Medical Center in Seattle Washington, who did such a wonderful job, putting me back together.

A special thanks to the man and woman who got inside my truck at the moment of the accident. Without them, I may not have made it to the path of recovery.

And naturally I thank my ex-wife, Monica, for your support through all those years of therapy.

Thanks to my primary doctor, Robert Audell, who did such a wonderful job helping me through all those years of therapy.

A thank you to my psychologist, Dr. Hirsh, who worked on the mental anguish.

I also want to say thank you to all those truck drivers who supported me before and after the accident.

Thanks to my boss at that time of the accident, Wilson (Cali Cali).

Also I want to Paty Paty, and Glenda Arias for your support.

I would especially like to thank Earl Ofari Hutchinson, who I know, without a doubt, was put into my life for a reason. You have been an inspiration to my life since the date I met you. But most of all, I want to thank you for helping me, put this book together.

Thank you to Fanon Hutchinson, for taking your time and making the promotional video.

Thanks to Yvonne Hutchinson, for editing my book.

Thank you to Alan Bell, for doing the book cover.

I also want to say thanks to all of those who helped me in putting this book together who are too numerous to name—you know who you are—I appreciate you all.

Introduction

The Search for the Promised Land

It was just like any other day. I was traveling in my eighteen-wheeler on I-90, approximately fifty miles east of Seattle, Washington. Little did I know that I was heading toward death.

I don't remember too much about the accident, except that I crashed into another truck at a speed of approximately 55 miles per hour. That day my life changed completely.

Medics loaded my broken body into a helicopter. I felt as if I was taking my last breath. Through the unbearable pain, I thought, "My kids, my family. I'm never going to see them again!"

I knew I was dying, but I didn't want to die alone. Death looked me in the eye more than once during those days that I lay in the hospital. I knew my life was never going to be the same. Terrified, I did not know what the future held.

I woke up in the hospital talking to myself.

When I was a child, all I had on my mind was running, jumping, playing, like any normal kid. I enjoyed going to school and having fun with my friends. But one day that changed, and just like that, my family had to make a very difficult decision. We would have to leave our home and travel to the United States for our own safety. At first, I didn't understand. I was just an innocent child. Why did we have to leave? My family was in danger from some people who didn't even know us. Who were they? Why did *they* want to hurt us?

Questions, Questions, Questions. But what were the answers? The search for those answers in my life was the beginning of a journey that would take me from a childhood in the then war torn, impoverished country of El Salvador, to what I and my parents saw as a land of hope and dreams for a better life, the United States.

It has been a journey filled with ups and downs, joy and pain. *Comeback: One Man's Triumph Over a Near Death Experience* is my story of that journey, a journey of hope and inspiration.

My mother said she had to move to another country. She left during the night, so we would not see her crying. I couldn't stop crying. I missed her so much. Where is my father? Why is he not with me? My grandma was taking care of us, but it was not the same without my mother. I wondered if I'd ever see her again.

1

The Promised Land?

I was born in 1968, in El Salvador in a small village, with no doctors or nurses around, just a lady helping my mom. I had a brother who was born before me, but he died when my mom was pregnant with me. He was about a year old when he died.

After I was born, my mom had another baby in 1971, my sister Marina. She had a different father, but just like my father, Marina's father did not live with our mother. My mom was single and living with her parents. She was a hardworking woman, when she was young; we were blessed to have a mother like her.

My parents separated when I was about a year and a half old. I remember meeting my dad twice in ten years, once when I was about five years old and then again when I was about ten. One time he tried to snatch me from my mom. I remember her crying and running behind him begging, "Please let him go." He took off without me that time, but little did we know he would try again.

My father used to work constructing roads. It happened that one day he found himself near our house, so he decided to kidnap me. But when he returned to the job site, his co-workers told him to take me back to my mother or else. He hurried up and took me back home.

I grew up in a house made of mud brick and roof tiles. We had no glass windows, just a piece a cloth or wood to cover the windows, no air conditioning, no electricity, just an oil lamp. No bedrooms, just a big living room and some sheets to separate the beds.

Around the year, 1975, our whole family, my mother, sister, my grandmother, and grandfather moved to the village of San Francisco Guajoyo.

Our house was near the main road.

My grandmother was an amazing, hardworking lady, a quality she passed on to my mom. Grandma cooked the best tamales. My grandpa took me to the fields where we grew corn and other vegetables. When he died in 1976, I was devastated because he was the man, I had called Dad since I was a little boy. Losing our grandpa really hit everyone very hard because he was the head of the house.

My grandpa had made this special machete for me, and when he died, I kept that machete until the day I left my country. I also remember that he had a favorite horse. When he went out to visit his friends or relatives, the two of us rode the horse, singing a song over and over until we reached the place where we were going.

* * * * *

When we moved to San Francisco, my mom opened a small store on the side of the main road. She worked hard. She would do anything to support me and my sister. She went to the big city and bought merchandise to sell at her little store. After my grandpa died, she had to make sure we were always okay.

The place where we lived before, we moved to town was far away from the main road, so when my grandpa was alive, he made sure we were always in his sight. Now that was my mother's responsibility. She had to work even harder than before. She got up very early in the morning to get everything ready for us and then went to her store. Sometimes we slept in the store because she was afraid someone might break in and steal her merchandise. I usually got up in the morning and helped her set up the store.

My mom was everything to me—father and mother. I don't remember ever seeing another man in her life until I came to this country. She was (and still is) my role model.

I think I can say for sure, we lived a decent life. We never went to bed hungry, unless it was because we would go out and play and come home late, past dinner time. Then we knew we were going to bed without eating. Nobody was going to feed us at night just because we decided to stay out late and play. But we did not care. We were kids in a beautiful country and a beautiful little town with some beautiful people. Growing up in a place like this was amazing.

We were friends with everybody. When there was an event, the whole town would show up and just have fun. We had no police station. Instead we had a group of people who were like a neighborhood watch. They carried machetes and patrolled the neighborhood. People saw police only when there was a truly dangerous situation.

While almost all of the adults worked in the fields, as kids, we went out to the soccer field after school and played until dark.

Every year, when it was corn season, in our town there lived lady name Sofia who made the best quesadillas bread in town. I helped her shuck the corn, and she gave me free quesadillas. She had a lot of daughters. I used to like Yolanda, one of her daughters even though she was a few years older than I was. There were big worms in some of the corn. I had fun chasing Yolanda around the house, and threatening to put the worms on her.

One time while I was walking down the road, I saw a big truck. One of the men inside looked very familiar. Then I heard someone call my name, and there he was, my father, Armando. Again! When I saw him,

I ran really fast to the house because I thought he was there to take me away with him. He stayed for like a whole day with us, and that was the last time I saw my father until I was grown.

It was not easy, growing without a father. I really missed him. I wanted badly to get to know him. Even though I was afraid of him because he wanted to take me away from my mother, I still wanted to be around him.

I knew that my father had other children and that I had a lot of brothers and sisters. I wanted to get to know them, but it was not my choice. My mom told me later, when I was a little older, the reason why she and my father split up. I envied other kids who lived with both of their parents, and I felt sad because I longed to live with both my parents.

*   *   *   *   *

Life was beautiful around this time, but things were about to change and not for the better. There were rumors that a war was about to start in El Salvador, a civil war. Of course, at that age I did not know what war was. People were saying that an army of guerillas were going to take all the twelve-year old boys to fight as soldiers in the war. They said it was not a choice, that everyone would be forced to join them. To save us, my mother decided to leave us with my grandmother while she went to the United Sates to work and make money enough to bring me and my sister to this country.

She assured us that everything was going to be okay. She said that she was moving so that we could have a better life. "I don't want a better life," I cried. "All I want is to be with you." In my young mind, I already had a wonderful life. But that night she left, without saying good bye. As I was sleeping, I felt someone kissing me. I didn't know it was my mother, saying good bye.

When I woke up in the morning, she was not in bed. "Where is my mom?" I asked Grandma,

She started crying. I thought maybe Mom was at her store down the street, but when I ran down to the store, it was closed, and there was nothing inside. I thought maybe she went to the city to buy groceries, and she would come back later. I waited all day, but she did not come. When night arrived and she had not come home, I noticed my uncle was not there either. Then I knew she was gone.

"Grandma, did my mom leave us?" I asked.

She replied, "Yes, but it's for the best. We will see her soon."

That day I refused to eat. I just wanted my mother to come back.

My sister was four years younger than me; she did not understand what was happening, so I suffered the most. It took me a while to understand what was happening. I thought the United States of America was close to my house and that I could take a bus and go visit my mother. Eventually I realized that she had gone some place very far away.

One day while playing with my friends, someone came and got me. I was told go home where a surprise awaited me. When I got home, I couldn't believe my eyes there she was, my mom with my uncle. "Mom!" I jumped on her and told her how much I loved her. I was so excited to see her. "Mom, please don't ever leave us again," I begged.

My mom told us that they had been sent back from Mexico. I had no idea where Mexico was, but I did not care, I was just happy to see her. Then I noticed something was wrong. She did not open her little store. I asked her when she was going to open her store and she just looked at me and said, "Son, I have to try to get to the United States again, so we are leaving soon again."

"No, Mom. You can't go again. Why can't you just open the store and let me help you? Don't leave, please!"

After that day, I was afraid that one morning I would wake up and find her gone again. Every morning the first thing I did was to check her bed. I was so happy when I saw her lying there asleep. Unfortunately, one day, she was not there. This time I didn't have to ask my grandmother. I already knew she was gone again. For the next few weeks, I would imagine that she was going to come back, like the first time. About a month later, I was told that she had made it to the United States. I remember I cried a lot, and I thought I would never see her again.

There were already rumors that the war in El Salvador was about to begin. My grandma was terrified because she did not want anything to happen to us.

However, the threat of danger did not stop me and my friends from going fishing or hunting or having fun. Acting as if we didn't have a care in the world, we went fishing really far away from the town. We caught a lot of fish.

When we got home late that night, I knew Grandma would be wide awake, waiting for me, and there she stood in front of the door with a big stick in her hand. As she raised the stick, I said," Grandma, look at all the fish I caught. Please don't hit me! Just look inside my fishing bag!"

She hugged me really hard and warned, "I don't care how many fish you catch. Don't you ever stay out this late again! Don't forget that animals can kill you, but most of all; I don't want nobody taking you away from me. What am I going tell your mom if something happens to you? You are going to give us both a heart attack. Don't you ever do that again?"

* * * * *

Things started changing in my country. We heard on the news that people had been found dead. People whispered about a group called the *Death Squad* that was killing citizens. Suddenly we began seeing a lot of soldiers in huge trucks driving back and forth on the main road. Not knowing any better at first, I was impressed by the sight. I thought it was cool to fight and kill the *bad guys*. But just *who were* the bad guys? I didn't have a clue.

I looked at the faces of some of the soldiers. I realized that they were very young—too young to be fighting in a war. They looked like they were no more than fifteen years old. When we watched the news, I realized that some of the guerillas *were* kids. Even scarier, those kids looked like they were *my age* and their rifles were almost as tall as they were. Looking at their faces, anyone could see that they were scared.

Finally, the army officially arrived in full force in our village. According to the rumors, they were assigned to protect a bridge that was near the town. On one occasion when I walked to the bridge, one of the soldiers declared, "Pretty soon you will be old enough to join the army, and if you refuse, the guerillas will come and take you and your friends by force. If you resist, they will kill you!"

One morning there was a battle not too far away

from us. We heard shooting, which seemed to be about a couple of miles away from our town. I was really scared. I was crying and fearful because I thought they were coming to attack our town.

A few days later, my grandma went to visit my mother's sister who lived in another village very far away. That night when we arrived at my aunt's house, we heard the sound of shooting not far from there. That night we slept outside on the mountain nearby because the house was next to a road. We returned to the house in the morning and stayed for a few more days. Then we went back home to my grandmother's house.

Another time, while my friend Miguel and I were fishing, we saw a whole bunch of soldiers. We just started running and did not stop for almost a half an hour. Why run away from men who were supposed to be protecting us? Because people had told us horrible stories about them. We didn't know who to trust. The soldiers fought the guerillas who were trying to take power away from the government. The guerillas fought to liberate us from the corrupt (?) government. It was confusing, but danger threatened us from both sides. My mother was right. It was time for us to leave El Salvador.

* * * * *

We used to go the city, Metapan, to call to America so we could talk to my mom. Whenever we talked, she always reassured me, "Don't worry son, just wait a little longer and I am going to bring you and you and your sister here." Despite the fact that I was glad to hear from her, I always cried after I finished talking with her. I missed my mom so much.

Now the situation in our country was getting worse. For that reason, Grandma told Mom to hurry and get us out of the country because it was getting more and more dangerous for me.

On our first attempt to come to America, money was paid to a man to escort me and a cousin, but he abandoned us when we got to Tecun Uman, Guatemala. We had no money and no food. We were able to get help from some cousins who sent us money to take a bus back to El Salvador. Almost right after that, we tried again, this time with a more honest escort, and finally landed in America.

2

A New Home,
A New Life

Ever since I was a young child, I had heard stories about the United States, how beautiful it is. Finally, I made it here and reunited with my mom, but I was heartbroken because my sister and my grandma remained in El Salvador. By now, conflict in our country had grown more and more violent. Besides my family, I had also left my friends behind, and I didn't know if I was ever going to see them again.

This country, America, was much more different than mine. When I came here, my mom was living with Jose'. He was a real cool guy, but at my age, I was not about to call him *Dad*. The three of us lived in a single apartment, and I used to sleep in the closet. My mother explained, "Life here is not like people think it is back in El Salvador. I have to work really hard, so for right now we live in this small apartment. It is small, but this is all we can afford right now."

I wanted her to know that I did not mind sleeping in a closet if it meant that I could be with the ones I love. "Mom, don't worry, I am just happy that I am here with you. I just want you to bring my sister here."

For a while I did not go to school because I was afraid to go by myself. It was too far away. There was no school bus, and Mom could not take me because she had to work. Eventually we moved to a building where my aunt lived so I could go to school with my cousins. We took the school bus together. Even though I was excited at first, I struggled with the school work, and I often cried because I could not understand what the teacher was saying.

I told my mom about my problem, and she promised me that she was going to go to school and talk to my teacher. Before she got a chance to take off from work to visit the school, Aunt Tina found me weeping by the stairs. "Why are you crying?" she asked.

I told her that I did not want to go school because the lessons were too hard and I did not understand what the teachers were saying. She went to school with me the same day and spoke to the school administrator. After that, they placed me in some lower classes.

I made new friends who also told stories about El Salvador. Some kids who were from other countries, such as the Honduras and Guatemala, also had their own stories. On the other hand, I didn't like to talk about the things that I saw. I just wanted to forget because every time I thought about that war, I thought about grandmother, my sister, my cousin, and my friends.

We heard about the horrible things that were happening in El Salvador on the news. One thing that was on my mind was where is my father? Is he still alive? Was I ever was going to meet him? I had been told that he lived in the big city of San Salvador and that I had some relatives on his side here in the United State, but I did not know where they lived.

* * * * *

My cousins Marcos and Mike we used to hang around and play basketball at the school yard. Occasionally, I saw a man with long hair lurking nearby. Sometimes he would come and play with us, but most of the time he just stood around. One day I saw him marking graffiti on the walls on the other side of the school. I saw him maybe ten times. I don't think I ever spoke to him that much. We might have exchanged words a few times, but I don't think I ever carried on a full conversation with him.

We met a man, whose name I have forgotten, who was my father's friend in El Salvador. He said that Dad was still alive. He suggested that I send him a letter. I was excited to learn that he was still alive. He gave me my dad's address. I wrote to him right away. He answered quickly and sent me a whole bunch of people's names, addresses, and phone numbers for members his family who were living in here in the United States. To my surprise, one address was just three blocks from where we lived.

My mother and I went to this address. According to my father, this was where two of my brothers lived. A man answered when we knocked on the door. Surprisingly, he recognized Mom and then looking at me, he exclaimed, "Hey, Pivi!" That was the nickname they had given me when I was a baby.

My mom, said to him, "Your name is Salvador, right?

He nodded, "Yes, it is."

What struck me was that Salvador looked familiar; I know I had seen him somewhere. I said, "I know you!"

He looked at me. "Hey! I know you too."

I realized, "You are the guy who sometimes hangs around the school yard. I saw you drawing graffiti on the walls on the other side of the school once."

"Yes, that was me," he confessed. But I don't do that no more."

I explained to my mom that I knew him. The three of us cried with happiness at seeing one another after so many years. Amazingly, here I was in front of someone who turned out to be an older brother on my dad's side. We had played basketball together, and we had no idea that we had the same father.

It was amazing that this guy, who hung around the basketball court, was my blood, my brother. That same day, I met another brother, Jorge. He told me about our other brothers that he knew of. He claimed that our father probably had more kids besides us, but he wasn't telling anybody about them.

At first, I was angry at my mother and father for this situation. How come my family was so divided that I didn't even know I had siblings? My mom told me the whole story of how my father used to be. Apparently, he really loved women and had trouble staying faithful to just one person. Even after she told me all of this, I did not resent him. I still wanted to meet my dad, who I had only seen twice in my life time. My mom told me that she had stayed with him until I was about one and half years old and that is why I had no memory of him or my brothers. She had left him when she was pregnant by me, but decided to give him a second chance. Unfortunately, it did not work out and she left him again.

Life can be strange sometimes. According to rumors, my father had about twenty kids. I guess this is the side effect of having a father who liked to play around. I had family I would probably never get to know, but I kept in touch with my new-found brothers until the day they left this country. Later, I met some more relatives from my father's side of the family.

* * * * *

Meanwhile I wasn't doing well in school. I knew I was not going to graduate, so I decided to stop going. I dropped out and started working.

I began staying out all night or not coming home at all. I was not listening to my mom. She gave me advice, which I proceeded to ignore. She cried a lot. She worried when I did not come home at night. I never called to let her know I was okay.

I wouldn't listen to my mother or anybody else. I was young, and I thought I had my whole life in front of me. I did whatever I wanted to, and I did not care about the consequences. My life had changed. I was no longer an innocent kid. I had a dark side that my family had not seen.

Until this day, some of them don't know the details about the things I did.

It was not that my mom was not involved in my life, but it was impossible for her to know what I was doing when I stayed away from home so much. Even though I hid my actions from her, she had a feeling something was wrong. My mother knew I was up to no good because of unsavory people I associated with.

I hated seeing her so sad. I wanted to change, but I did not know how.

Some nights when I stayed in my car, I heard a voice scolding me, "Douglas, what are you doing here? You have a place to stay. Go home!"

One night I was listening to a song when I heard a strange voice that told me to take my own life and just get it over with. It mocked me, "Nobody loves you. No one cares whether you live or die." That made me cry, and right then I wished I had somebody to talk to.

Around this time, sister arrived. My mom and I were very excited to see her,

But we still worried about my grandmother, who was still in El Salvador.

Mom seemed to think that my sister's coming might cause me to start being more responsible. She thought helping her with my sister would stop me from disrespecting her rules. But it didn't. I kept right on doing whatever the hell I wanted.

I was out of control by now. I did something horrible. Even though I know God has already forgiven me, until this day, it still haunts me. My mom and I were arguing. It happened so many years ago that I don't remember what we argued about, but I am pretty sure is was not because I was a good boy. But one thing I never will forget. When I started to leave the house, she tried to stop me. I pushed her so hard that she landed on the floor. She broke down crying, "Douglas, what have you done? God is going to punish you!"

At that moment, I didn't care. I left the house and didn't look back. I think that was the night when I heard the voice urging me to take my own life. A lot of people thought I was taking drugs. I never did drugs, so it wasn't drugs that

twisted my mind. In fact, I think I have only smoked weed about ten or so times all my life. No, I was doing something else. I belonged to a group of young teens who worshipped Satan. It was a satanic group, but we pretended it was bigger than people thought. At this point, I need to clarify something. I never hurt another human being physically; nor did I ever hurt any animals. but under this bad influence, I did hurt the love of my life— my mother.

As a member of this cult, I was taught that when I died, I was going to be rewarded by Satan with a special place in hell. Today when I think about it, it sounds ridiculous that I would even want such a thing, but at the time I was fascinated with the whole idea.

Hanging around with this groups of teens and seeing the things they used to do and practice, was getting to me. There where times when I would lie on my bed or sofa. "I would close my eyes and see my myself floating in the air and then looking down and I would see my body lying down". There were times that I thought I was sleeping and I was a nightmare, buy after a while I realized I was actually awake.

One time, I was asked by a friend if I would drive him and another guy somewhere to get a car. When we arrived at the destination, I parked and waited for them at a nearby street corner. The police drove up and stopped and asked what I was doing there. I told them that I was waiting for some friends. They pulled me out of the car and handcuffed me. Right about that time, they saw my friend walking on the street and arrested him, too. The other guy got away. I was charged with Grand Theft Auto (GTA). Since it was my first time getting arrested, I was released the next day on my own recognizance.

The detective handling the case gave me some good advice. He told me to get my life straight or I would wind up doing something really stupid and going to jail for the rest of my life or getting killed. That advice stuck in my head for a while. After that day, I stopped hanging around friends who engaged in shady activities, but I continued to party at all hours of the night.

Then God started to work in my life the year of 1987. While working at a grocery store, as a cashier I saw a young woman who looked familiar. She was carrying a baby. It turned out to be Yolanda, the girl I had chased with the corn worms when I was a kid back in El Salvador. I did not see her again until November of that same year, while visiting my cousin who was married to her sister. I asked, "Are you single?"

"Yes." She replied. My heart leaped with joy.

On our first date, I wondered, "Do you remember when I used to chase you around the house with those worms?"

"How could I forget that? You were a little menace."

But I was no longer a playful kid. At nineteen years old, I considered myself a grown man. Around this time, she was looking for an apartment, and she asked me if I wanted to move in with her. I had told her that I was sleeping in my car. Of course, I agreed to move in with her. That made my mother happy because I no longer hung out on the street.

During the same month, she invited me to her church. Was this God's plan? The preacher, who conducted the services that night, spoke about a teenager in trouble. At first, I thought, someone had told him about me because I was in all kinds of trouble with the law and with my family. I felt he aimed his sermon directly at me. Especially, when he said, "Only Jesus Christ is the solution for all your troubles." *(Matthew 11:28)" Come to me, all you who are weary and burdened, and I will give you rest."* When I left church that night, I assumed the pastor said all those things personally to me because all the while he preached; he kept looking at me and smiling.

* * * * *

On a Friday night, January, 1988, Yolanda, now

my fiancée, asked me to accompany her to her job in Beverly Hills. Before I arrived at her house, the cops pulled me over and arrested me for receiving stolen property. They told me the seats in the car did not belong to the car. They were correct. They came from my cousin's car. He crashed his car and planned to junk it, so he gave me the seats. No matter how hard I tried to explain about how I got the seats, it fell on deaf ears. Was this God's plan?

When we got to jail, they gave me some bad news. I could not post bail because I had violated my probation for an offense that I had committed about a year ago. They told me I had to see a judge on Monday.

When they took me to the jail cell, I started remembering what that preacher said. I kept hearing voices in my head. "You are in big trouble. Why don't you try Jesus?" All my life, I heard about God, but all my life I thought God was just a myth. Because I once belonged to a group of young men who worshipped Satan, the idea that God existed struck me as unbelievable.

In those days, I thought that Satan was more powerful than this mythical God. But now I felt like my devotion to Satan had resulted in my life going down the drain. No help came from Satan. In fact, it was probably due to his influence that I now faced about a year in jail. Back in the day, I had done a lot of foolish things for him, and this might have been his way of paying me back.

As I lingered in jail that night, I remembered the time I thought about killing myself and all the nights I slept in my car. That was then, but this was now. I had a girlfriend and a decent place to stay. If I did not change my lifestyle now, I might not get another chance.

3

The Fall

I got down on my knees, and I prayed to the God, the God I once mocked as just a myth. I said to Him, "God if you are real, like the pastor said in church, I'm going to ask you for one favor. I want to be out of jail by tomorrow. If you do that for me, I'll give you my life." Of course, I knew I had asked for the impossible because I had just been told there was no bail and that I had to see the judge Monday. I think I prayed all night.

Before that, whenever someone tried tell me about God, I made fun of them. I did not need God in those days of my life. As a young guy, I didn't want hear about God. I didn't need Him. I had everything.

The next day was Saturday. A police officer came to my cell and told me that I had been bailed out. At first, I thought it was a joke, but he walked me to the front desk, and there stood my fiancé Yolanda with my mom and a friend. I left there quickly before someone discovered that they had made a mistake.

I told my Mom and Yolanda that while I was in jail, I had promised to give my life to Christ. I repeated what my jailers told me, that I had to see the judge on Monday, that there was no bail for me. I thought maybe my mother or Yolanda had pleaded my case and convinced them to give me bail this Saturday.

My mom was so excited to hear that I had given my life to God because she knew I was in all kind of trouble. I went to church that same night, and the pastor prayed for me and my fiancé. I asked God one more time, to please forgive me, that I needed Him. I needed my family to trust me again. I did not want my mom to worry about me anymore. I kept telling God, "I don't want to go to jail because I have a court date and things don't look good for me." Surprisingly, when I went to court, I was told that the charges were dismissed.

I still faced the charges for GTA, my previous case. Hallelujah! When I called the detective handling the case, he said not to worry; the charges against me had been dismissed. He told me to stay out of trouble. I informed him that I gave my life to Christ. I was going to church and no longer associating with people who were a bad influence. I stopped partying, also. He wished me good luck, I thanked him for his help, breathed a great sigh of relief, and began my life as a Christian.

My life became complete around June, 1988. My beloved grandma Leandra, arrived from El Salvador. I couldn't be happier. Rumors reached her in El Salvador about my not doing well here, but when she arrived in the United States, she found a different person. She found a man of faith, a man of God, who was married and expecting our first child. I told my grandma," You never have to worry about me ever again. I am a changed man.

We had our first child, Diana, in November, 1988. My grandmother was happy to meet her great, grand baby, and my mom was overjoyed to welcome her first grandchild.

By this time, I had started a new job working construction. A happily married man and happy father, I was active in church. I served as the youth president for a while. Every weekend we traveled to Tijuana. My pastor put me in charge of a small church.

One day, I saw a young man across the street right in front of where I lived. He looked very familiar. I went and talked to him, and to my surprise, it was one of the guys that I met a few years before. He looked different, very skinny. He told me that he was sick. He said also that he was homeless and sleeping on the streets. I invited him to come to church with me, but he refused. I offered him financial help. He refused that also. I told him that I was married, had a kid lived a wonderful life. A few months later, I saw him again, this time he looked worse

Again, I offered to help, and again he refused. I didn't see him for a while. About a year later, I learned that he was found unconscious or dead on the street. It hurt me a lot to hear that, but I had tried to help him. After I found out about his death, I told myself; that could had been me if had continued my ungodly life style.

In May of the year 1990, we had a second child, our son, Joshua. Later that year, my grandma made the decision to go back to EL Salvador. We tried to persuade her not go, but it was in vain. She told us that the war was almost over. She was feeling sick, and she wanted to die in her country so she could be buried next to her husband. We tried to convince her, to no use. Then we tried to convince her that if she died here, we would take her body back to El Salvador.

*   *   *   *   *

In 1990, one the most beautiful years of my life, my son Josh was born.

Also, in that same year, I went to El Salvador to reunite with my father. I was twenty-two years old, and I had been waiting for this moment for almost twelve years. Jorge and Salvador, the two brothers I had met in Los Angeles who had moved back to El Salvador, came to the airport with him to pick me up. I was glad to see them again.

Finally, I came face-to-face with the man who had once tried to kidnap me. My father was a tailor. He made me a whole bunch of pants and shirts. In fact, when I left EL Salvador, I packed more clothes than the ones I brought with me.

Visiting the country posed a danger because of the war which continued to rage, but I was able to meet my father's other children, my brothers and sisters. I spent the first week with my dad going to meet, not only his kids, but my aunts, nephews, and cousins. One meeting stands out. We went to the ocean at this beautiful place in El Salvador, La Costa Del Sol, where one of my sisters lived.

In addition to meeting my siblings and other relatives, I went to visit my grandma. the love of my life. She did not know I was coming, but she was excited to see me. She had moved away from the house where we used to live and gone to stay with one of my aunts.

I went to see my childhood friends, as well. Sadly, I received some bad news. One of my best friends who had joined the army, was murdered during a battle with the rebels. Additionally, some of the other guys I grew up with had joined the army and were still fighting the rebels.

Soon it was time for me to return to the big city

with my father; but before I left, I went to say good bye to all of my friends. I even went looking for the place where my mom used to have her little store. Alas, it was not there anymore. All I had left was memories of my childhood. I left our little town, wondering if I would ever see my grandma or my friends again.

When Dad came to get me, I told him to stop by these hill. I asked, "Do you remember this place?"

"Yes," he said. "This is the place where my co-workers stopped me when I tried to steal you from your mother."

I reminded him, "Sometimes, even though we don't understand why things happen, they do happen for a reason. Mom needed me more than you did. You already had a lot of kids. She only had me and my sister. What you did is in the past. This is the present. I'm glad we got together. I never hated you for not staying around. I did wish that you had stepped up when Mom left for the United States, but it was okay. I don't hold any grudges against you."

It was time to say goodbye. We hugged and cried, and I promised that I would come back to see him and the family every year. There were rumors that the war was about to be over and there was going to be peace agreement

I kept that promise and I visited him almost every year until 2000.

* * * * *

In 1991, I started a new job where I was I in supervised 112 apartment units and four other buildings. During October of the same year, we had our third child, Douglas. To my way of seeing it, my life was complete! I was going to church. I had a wonderful job, free rent. What could possibly go wrong?

Shortly after Douglas was born, my wife and I began having some disagreements, and we stopped going to church. I stopped praying and reading the Bible. I made up any excuse not to go to church. I imagined that I could fix our problems myself. Instead we started to argue more frequently, sometimes over nothing. I knew that my life and our marriage were falling apart, but I did not know why. We had been faithful to one another. We had some beautiful kids. We lived a fairly comfortable life. One thing I did notice. Neither one of us made an effort to do anything to save our marriage.

In March of 1992, we separated. My wife moved out of our home.

This was the last thing I wanted to happen. I did not want to live apart from my kids, I wanted to raise them together with my wife. I did not want them to go through what I had gone through, being raised without a father. This was killing me, but I didn't even have sense enough to ask God for help.

At the end of this same year, I had met another woman, who ended up getting pregnant. In 1993, my ex-wife became pregnant again. I was happy at first, but soon I lapsed into a deep depression, but I did not want anyone to know that I was getting sick.

By now, I had two women were pregnant by me. My mother worried about me. She kept insisting, "Douglas, you have to get back to God. Only He can help you. I have noticed that you have been drinking lately, and I don't remember you ever drinking before, not even when you were young and crazy. What is happening, son? "I wasn't drinking a lot, just once in a while, but my mom was worried because she had never seen me drink alcohol.

In June of 1993, my son Alex was born. I was not

living with his mother at that time. She and I were on and off all the time. We tried a few times to get together, but it never worked out. In December 1999, she finally decided she had had enough. She told me that if I was not going to get serious in our relationship, she was going to move on, and she left me for good.

*   *   *   *   *

That same year 1993, I went back to EL Salvador to see my father and grandmother. To my regret, that would be the last time I saw my grandma alive. When I left, she told me to take care of myself and to get back with God. She said, "I'm dying, so this will be the last time you see me. Take care of your babies and your mother. Don't make her suffer no more. You were such sweet boy. I know you went through a lot when you were young, but look at you now, all grown up and a father yourself."

I protested, "You are not dying yet, Grandma, but I want you to know that you are the best grandma in the whole world. You did so much for me and my sister. I am sorry for the days, I made you worry, when I used to come home late. I Do you remember that night I came home super late with all those fish?"

She laughed, "Those fish saved you from a big time whupping!"

"I know," I grinned. "I saw you getting ready to hit me with that big stick." I kissed her for the last time. I knew in my heart that I was not going to see her again. Sure enough, she died the same year. I was glad that I had seen her before she passed away.

Too many things happened to me in 1993. My son Alex had just been born. My ex-wife was pregnant. My grandma passed away. I didn't know what to do. Brothers from church came to visit me, and I would always tell them the same lie. "I will be back to church pretty soon. I just got to take care of a few things." I started having nightmares, horrible ones. I would wake up crying for no reason, and I was staring to lose weight. I realized I had to do something right away or my life would fall apart completely.

Then I found another way to spend my time. I started working out. When I started, I weighed 130 pounds. I have been skinny all my life, and now I found something worthwhile to do with my time, put

on some weight. This benefitted me because at that point in my life, things were not looking good. I was suffering from depression. My mother started to worry. I had already hurt her too much in the past, and I did not want to put her through that pain again.

To make matters worse, my ex-wife told me that she was moving to Portland, Oregon. When she moved, she was pregnant and that made me even more depressed. Life seemed overwhelming. Lifting weights served as my therapy during this time. In January, 1994, our daughter Hellen was born. I sent child support. I wanted to go and see my baby, but my ex told me not to come because she did not want to see me.

In 1995, I decided to go to Portland anyway to see my babies. I was very happy to see them. Hellen was gorgeous; she looked like her Aunt Marina, my sister. I only stayed for one day, because my ex-wife told me, it was better if I did not stay with her. I respected her decision, but I told her that I would not keep driving 1000 miles to spend only one day with my children.

4

Hitting the Road

In 1996, I made the decision to become a truck driver. One of the main reasons why I chose this profession was that it would allow me to work for a company and drive cross country. Another reason was that I felt that this could help me with my present situation. It would be good to get away for a while—to meet other people and see other places.

From the moment I came to America, I fell in love; to me everything was beautiful: the culture, the streets, the parks, the schools, the lakes, the mountains, the roads. I knew, too, that California was not the only place where I would encounter beauty. One of my biggest dreams was to go and see the rest of the country. I thought this was the perfect time to get away from the pressures of home. This would be my therapy, and I was going accomplish one of my biggest dreams—to travel across the United States.

On my first trip I went to New York. I was scared at first, but I didn't let fear stop me. I got lost big time. In fact, I think I spent more time trying to locate my destination than I did when I finally got there, but that didn't bother me. It was just as I imagined, the other states were also beautiful. The more I traveled the more excited I became.

When I arrived at my destination, I met another driver who worked for the same company. I told him about how I struggled just to get there. He said, "Not to worry, I will show you how to read a map." He got his truck loaded first. He was going to California, also, so he waited until I got loaded. Had it not been for him, who knows how long it would had taken me to get back to California? He also helped me to install a CB radio. Excited, I started talking to everyone on the radio. I told my new friend about why I had become a truck driver. He listened to my story with interest. Then he assured me, "You will love the rest of the country."

We stopped in Amarillo, Texas, at a restaurant where if someone could eat seventy-two ounces of meat in sixty minutes, it was free. He said he wanted to try it. I just ordered a burger. He tried, but he fell short, which cost him a lot of money

We finally arrived in Los Angeles. As he prepared to drop off his load, I thanked him for what he had done. From that day to this, I still get lost occasionally, but not like the first time. Knowing how to read a map made a big difference.

One time, I went to pick up a load from Denver, Colorado, that was coming to Los Angeles. As I came down the mountain on I 70, the brakes from my rear trailer caught on fire. Luckily, I was able to stop the truck. The truck was burning, but nobody stopped to help me from my side of the highway. Then I saw a truck headed in the opposite direction. The driver stopped and ran across the freeway, hauling three fire extinguishers. Between the two of us we were able to put the fire out.

This was the second "good Samaritan" I had met. He also showed me how to drive my truck on the lower gears going down the hill, and he taught me how to adjust the brakes from the trailer. I expected that I would more meet people like these two guys because I had heard how helpful most of the people were here in the United States.

* * * * *

In January of 1997, I was delivering a load to New York, during one of the worst snow seasons in history. I stopped in Denver and spent a day there with one of my best friends, Juan Carlos. After leaving Carlos, I continued my journey. About thirty miles East of St. Louis Missouri, on I-70, I had my first accident in the snow. It had been snowing all day. I wasn't even going fast. As the traffic

stopped in front of me, I stepped on the brakes. My cab slid to the other side of the freeway, but luckily nothing happened to me or the truck. I remember I just grabbed the steering wheel and prayed.

When I came to stop, I heard a driver on the CB radio, exclaiming, "Son, God had to be with you because you are driving a cab-over, and you know how easy it is for those trucks to flip over. "

I agreed, "Yes, God has must have been with me!"

I took some time off after the accident and tried to work locally, but I couldn't stand it. I really missed traveling the country, so I went back to working long distances across the states. This time I worked as a team. A friend of the family named Francisco had a truck, and he asked me to join him. By now, I knew the country by heart. I did not need a map to find the places I had to go. Besides, most of the time we traveled the same routes, from Los Angeles to Atlanta and from Atlanta to New Jersey and back home.

In 1997, when I got home from a trip from New York, my mom was waiting for me. She said, "I got a big surprise for you. Look inside the room." There stood my daughter Diana and my son Douglas. A while ago, their mother had asked me if I could help her by taking two of our kids because it was becoming too much for her to raise five children on her own. I had agreed, but she was just now getting around to sending them to me. I guess she wanted to surprise me. Boy, was I glad to see them! I had seen my daughter the year before, for just one day, but now they were going to be with me for a long time, if not forever.

Their mother and I had spoken about their staying until they were grown, but I was so happy to see them that I wanted them with me for the rest of my life. I knew it was not going to be easy because I was single at the time, and there was no one else who could stay with them while I was out on the road. I stayed at home with them for almost a month. I did not go to work. I enrolled them in school. My cousin's wife took care of them for a while when I went back to driving, but it was not easy. Little Douglas behaved terribly; he would not listen to anybody, and it was becoming a problem to take care of him. All that year, I stayed off from work most of the time to be with my children.

To complicate matters, the school notified me that I needed to get a letter from their mother if they were to continue going to our neighborhood school. I was told that it was better to get full custody since they already had been with me for more than six months. I filed the papers, and I was awarded full custody. Even though I was happy to finally have my kids with me, I faced a difficult situation. I might have to quit driving and find another job that would allow me to stay at home with the kids.

I contacted my father in El Salvador and explained my situation. I asked him how he felt about keeping the kids with him for a couple of years. He loved the idea. He said that it would be an honor to take care of his grandchildren, that it would make up for not being around to take care of me when I was there, so in 1999, I took them to El Salvador.

I really loved my job. I was getting paid for going on vacation every week. I traveled to many places and met wonderful people. I enjoyed interacting with the customers. People who worked in the stores where I made deliveries would call the company I worked for and request that the dispatcher assign me as their regular driver. I used to meet drivers, and some of them look depressed and seem to hate what they were doing. I used to wonder. How could you hate this kind of job? We are making money while we travel. We are delivering merchandise that people need, and we are part of this country's economy." I told everybody, "I love what I do! One day I am going to buy myself a big truck with a big cabin and just drive across country and spend my life traveling the road."

* * * * *

One day while I backed my truck into a gate, I saw a young man through my review mirror who looked like he was having a bad morning. I got out and went to the back of the store and knocked on the door. He opened the door and asked me, "What do you want?"

I told him, "I noticed you are by yourself, and I've left a lot of merchandise. I'd like to help you put it away." He was amazed. "You want to help me?" He told me that most of the truck drivers who drop off their loads don't like to help. In fact, some never even offer.

"Yes," I told him. "I need to do some exercise, and this will be a good work out for me. My muscles are hungry, so I need to feed them!" I made him laugh with that joke. While we worked, I gave him some advice. "You should smile a little more, or is it just today that you are having a bad morning?" He said he

was tired of that job. I remember telling him, ""
Well, you can always look for another job, a job that you like, but while you are looking for another job, you have to enjoy this one."

He asked if I enjoyed my job. I answered, "My friend, I don't just enjoy this job; I'm getting paid for doing what I love and for going out on vacation every week and meeting people like you and most of all, I meet women!" "Furthermore," I told him, you have to enjoy life and be thankful that you have a job. You should wake up in the morning and come to work with a smile on your face. You might just change someone's life with a smile."

But I did tell him that I don't always help people unload or load the trailer. In some places, it was too much work, and we are not allowed inside their buildings. But wherever I can, I do lend a hand. When we were finished unloading the trailer, my new young friend was a totally different person. He was all smiles.

About a week later, I was told by the dispatcher that someone had called the company to inquire if it was possible for me to be their regular driver. It came from the store where I had helped the young guy. I went back again to that store, and he was there. This time he was smiling from the time he opened the gates. He told me that somebody had called the company and asked for me to be their regular driver, and they had told them, they were going to try, but they had the same request from other stores. I promised that I would make an effort to come to his store as often as I could.

* * * * *

Around 1999, I decided to stay local for a while, just driving the West Coast, California, Oregon, and Washington. Every once in a while, I would make a cross country run just to keep in shape.

Some truck drivers give themselves nick names or other drivers like to give you one. I loved panthers, so I started calling myself "Panther," but one day another driver said he was really mad at me for using that name. According to him, his compadre was the original panther on the I-5, freeway and in California.

I guess drivers here in California really love their nick names and take them very seriously.

My boss Francisco was with me that day and overheard the guy on the radio. He shouted, "Hey you! You can keep that name. we don't want it!"

I objected, "Boss, wait! Don't give my name away. Don't forget I have a panther tattoo in my right arm."

Panther was my nick name before I became a truck driver."

"I have the perfect name for you," My boss told me. "You look really good, and you take care of yourself, so I going to name you, Super Pollo (Super Chicken). Francisco gave me this name because he had seen a cartoon character where a chicken hawk is chasing a dog and a rooster. In one of the episodes, the chicken hawk was lifting weights to make him strong enough to catch the rooster and the dog.

"Okay, Boss, why? That was a baby hawk not a chicken." He told me that I looked like the cartoon character because I had a big chest, big arms, big legs, but no butt, and to him that hawk looked like a little chicken. I could not change his mind. From that day on I was called "Super Pollo."

One day, I met a guy with very interesting voice, and for almost five hours, I thought I was talking to a woman. To my surprise it turned out to be a guy. Later I found out that this guy was a cousin of my boss, and we ended up working as a team for a while.

I decided to try and fake my voice, too. Like magic, I began imitating the voice of a woman, but now I needed another nick name. Some of my buddies were really excited to lay one on me. I used to dye my hair different colors. One day, I arrived at the company with red hair. One of my friends crowned me with the nick name "Caperusita Roja" which means, Little Red Riding Hood. And no matter how much I tried to disown the name, it stuck. Now I had two nick names. I used to tell jokes over the radio, so I had a group of fans who would call and ask me to either wait for them at the truck stop or they would wait me, so we can ride together.

Not everyone liked me; some drivers cursed at me. I never cursed back. Instead I tried to piss them off even more by continuing to speak in my female voice. *(These two nicknames would come to play a big part after the accident when I came home)*

Soon my little impersonation sparked some real anger. A woman started cursing at me over the radio. She sounded very annoyed. Apparently, she really thought that I was a woman. I was about to have some fun with this lady, but then I recognized a voice over the radio. It was a guy we call Renegado. He said, "Don't pay attention to my wife, Baby. She's just jealous.

Now that I knew who she was, I knew what I had to do next. I said, "Listen to me, honey, it is not my fault that you are probably over weight and ugly and your man has to come all the way here because he wants to be with a real woman."

What she said next, I can't write in this book. I replied, "Sorry, honey, but it's not my problem that your man likes sexy women like me. Then I think her husband must have taken the radio away from her because, after that, I did not hear from her again.

Another time, me and a driver, Pupuso, also known as Marimar, were driving on the Grape vine. We were just having fun. He was in his truck, and I was in mine.

When, suddenly, out of the nowhere, this voice came on the radio. threatening us. "If only I had the chance to have you guys in front of me, I would cut both of you guys' pipi." Of course, he said "pipi" using other words. When I looked to my left, I saw a guy talking on his radio. I called my friend over the phone and told him, "I just saw the guy who wanted to cut off our pipis."

He had just got off at the same place where we

were getting off. I asked Marimar if he would help me play a joke on him, but it required us to act like girls in person and outside of the truck. He said, "No way!"

I pleaded with him, "Come on, Marimar, you have to back me up on this one. "He asked me if I was sure. "What can we lose?" I asked. "He can't beat up both of us, and I don't see a machete. Please, you have to."

He gave in, "Okay, yes."

I saw Marimar getting in line to order a sandwich from a subway, so I lifted up my shirt and tied a knot in it, and as soon as I got close to him, I spoke in the same female voice I did on the radio. "Marimar, I am so worried, honey, because I smell death; I smell fear. I am scared, baby. I don't know, but I have this feeling, that the man who was coming down the Grape Vine, I think he is here. I can smell his machete.

This guy looked at me and looked at my friend. He said, "Please don't tell me you are those guys that were making those voices." You might think by now, that I would talk in a normal voice, now that he knew who we were, but no, I went all the way and maintained my "feminine side." Marimar, on the other hand, just couldn't handle it. He just started laughing.

Me, I kept on going. "Mister, are you that guy who wants cut our pipi? Because I don't have one anymore. I already took it off myself." He looked at me and laughed. "I really thought you were gays." I told him that we weren't gay, but that there was nothing wrong with being gay and a truck driver. He asked us which way we were going. We told him we were headed to the Bay Area.

He asked if he could ride with us. We were more than glad to say, yes, because his life was about change. Most truck drivers recognized each other by their trucks, and, of course by their nicknames. So, it was just the three of us all the way to the bay area, and every time some asked who was driving the third truck, he gave his nickname, and he claimed he was our body guard.

About three hours into our drive, someone said, "Hey is that you Caperusita Roja and Marimar? I can see my two my favorite girls are going the other way, but who is the third driver behind you? So, this guy, who just hours before wanted to cut our pipis, said the most hilarious thing I had ever heard. He said, with a sexy lady's voice. "Excuse me, but it's three of us now."

I laughed so hard, and Marimar came on the radio and said, "Man, it took only three hours to convert this guy into one of us. He responded, "Not really. I just did not know how to come out."

When we said goodbye, he said something that got my attention. "You are an amazing person with a great sense of humor. It has been a pleasure meeting you and your friend, Marimar.

I answered, "You know why I am like this? Because I don't see this a job, I see this as an adventure, and I love what I do, and I love making people laugh, and I love been on the road."

Not everything was that cool while on the road. Once, as I was pulling out of a parking spot, I almost hit a truck. The driver cursed me. I apologized to him, and out of the nowhere, he started yelling, You (expletive) Mexican! You shouldn't be driving. Go back to Mexico! That's probably where you got your license from!".

I just kept driving. As I pulled out of the truck parking lot, I saw an African American guy by the exit. He made eye contact with me and smiled. Then he got on his radio and went off on the racist driver. He asked the guy, "Do you want to get out of the truck and take care of business with me?"

He radioed me, "Don't worry, my Mexican brother, I will take care of this big mouth." By that time, I was on the freeway. I think it was really cool of him to do that. That was not the only time I had this kind of encounter with some drivers that kept sending me to Mexico. The only problem was, I am not from Mexico. But I did not care because these people were just a few compared to all of the beautiful people I met while traveling around the country.

* * * * *

By the end of 2000, I went to EL Salvador, to pick up my kids Diana, 14, and Douglas, who had just turned 10. Their mother told me she wanted them back and that now I could come and visit them anytime I wanted. Her giving me permission made it okay that she wanted to take them back.

Meanwhile, I had another accident in December, 2000. My truck caught on fire. Fortunately, I was only going five to ten miles per hour when it happened, so nothing happened to me. Then I had another accident in April 2001. A car cut me off, and to avoid hitting the car, I stepped on the brakes and moved to the right shoulder. I ended up on the side of the road on a ditch. The truck jack knifed, but once again, I escaped without a scratch. Nothing happened to me, but the truck had some damage.

In December 2000. I started dating someone new. After a few months, we decided to move in together. By June 2001, my ex-wife sent Douglas back to me again. She really loves our son, but he was too much for her to handle at that time. During the first months of his stay, my girlfriend was helping me with him, while I was driving. But in September 2001, she moved with her parents to Washington State.

While she was gone, Douglas' aunt was helping me, but still I cut back on my work schedule a lot. In January, 2002, I convinced my girlfriend to come back to live with me. She resumed the task of helping me with Douglas, so I could work more. Meanwhile, she announced that she was pregnant!

In December 2002, my ex-wife told me again that she wanted Douglas back. He was eleven years old, and she thought maybe she'd be able to handle him now. I drove Douglas to Oregon, and on my way there, my girlfriend, who was almost nine months pregnant, called and told me that she was having contractions and she was on her way to the hospital. By the time I got to Portland, she called me with the news that the baby had been born. I was so disappointed and angry that I had missed my son's birth. That day I did not sleep at all. I drove back to Los Angeles and went directly to the hospital. My son had some complications because he was born premature, almost a month early. To make matters worse, my girlfriend and I were not getting along. Sometimes I stayed in my truck and slept there. I lied and told her that I was working because I did not want come home and fight with her. We broke up in April, 2003, she left once again to live with her parents in Washington.

5

At Death's Door

In May, 2003, I learned a lesson that I will remember the rest of my life. I was asked to take a load to Tacoma, Washington. At first, I was excited because on my way there, I could stop in Portland and see my kids. For some reason, I had this strange feeling that something was going to happen. My happiness turned into desperation, and it was so strange that I started writing a letter to my daughter. I asked my daughter to please forgive me for not being there for them when they needed me the most and to tell her brothers the same thing, to forgive me. Why I was writing this, I didn't know at the moment, but I was about to find out.

It was like it was meant to be. It was like the only way to stop me. If we only knew in advance what was going to happen to us in the future, we might be prepared. I had dreams about this day, but it never crossed my mind that those dreams were about to become real. I have seen multiple accidents in which truck drivers have died. Some of them were my friends. Now I was about have my own accident, but I did not know, it was going to be so big. My catastrophe not only changed my life, but the life of those around me.

From March, 1992, until May 23, 2003, I ran away from God, but He never ran away from me. I hid from Him, but He never hid from me. I left Him, but He never left me. I had three close calls with death in those three accidents.

I took a load to Tacoma, Washington in May, 2003. That trip was not like the other ones I had done in the past. I was taking a set of doubles (front and back trailers, linked together), something that I had not liked to do in the past. I left Bakersfield, California, May 21. When I got to Fresno, I saw an accident on the other side of the freeway. It was a set of doubles, just like mine. The rear trailer had separated from the front trailer, and it was on the side of the road. I immediately sent a message to my dispatcher, telling him that I was scared, and I felt like a chicken. Something was not right in me.

I arrived in Corning, California on the same day. I slept there for eight hours. On Thursday, the twenty-second, I woke up around 4 a.m. I turned the radio on, only to hear that an accident had happened near the state line of Oregon and California, and the freeway was closed. I figured that I was still three hours away from there and by the time I arrived at the site of the accident, the freeway would be open. But to my surprise, the freeway was still closed around 7 a.m. when I got there.

I heard on CB radio that the freeway was closed for so long time because the truck driver probably had died in the crash. Some truckers were saying, it was a single-vehicle accident, and that fact stayed on my mind all the way to Tacoma the next day.

I made it to Portland on the same day. I met with my kids and took my son Josh out to celebrate his birthday, which was only five days away. I bought him a couple of pair of shoes. We talked for a few hours. He was doing well in school. He said he was going to be a professional basketball player. He declared that one day he was going to "be really rich," and he was going to buy me and his mom each a house, and we would never have to work again. I told him that I was proud of him.

I went to sleep, and woke up at 5 a.m. I drove to Tacoma and dropped a set of doubles and picked up a regular 53-footer. I got on freeway I-90 and continued east. Around 10:30 a.m., on that day, May 23, I called my ex-girlfriend, my son's mother. She told me that Matthew was crawling now. We talked about getting back together. We started making plans to get married and discussed how to make our marriage work. I was very happy that at least she was thinking about our getting back together.

Around 11:00 a.m., approximately by mile marker, fifty-one, on I 90, I remember seeing a red truck, and then right after that, I don't remember anything else. I was told that I rear-ended a truck carrying a shipment of apple concentrate. According to witnesses, I hit the other truck with such strong force that people thought it the collision occurred while it was parked. What actually caused the collision was the driver moving too slow and changing lanes. Other witnesses said that I was following too close, but I was going uphill. I was not speeding. However, the impact was so severe that the engine of my truck was almost completely pushed inside the cabin. The dashboard smashed into me, breaking my right leg in several places.

* * * * *

I remember being trapped inside the cabin of the truck, screaming and begging the people that appeared outside the truck, probably onlookers, "Please! Get me out of this truck." The pain was devastating. My head was bleeding, and I could feel something was wrong with my chest. I was stuck between the steering wheel and the seat, and I couldn't move.

People were yelling for somebody to get me out of the truck because it had caught on fire. I thought I was going to burn to death. Then I heard someone say, "No it's not fire. It's just the steam from the radiator." A woman got inside the cab, and some of the bystanders told her she needed to get out because the truck might catch on fire. She refused, "No, I need to assist him.

I'm a certified nurse, and I want to secure his neck."

Another good Samaritan, a man, appeared. He got inside the truck to help her. I asked him, "Can you please find my Bible?"

He said, "Everything has fallen out of your truck. What do you need?"

I told him, "I want to pray. I want my Bible. I want to ask God for forgiveness" I knew something was terribly wrong. I had this weird sensation of something hot inside my chest. I felt like I was dying.

The stranger grabbed my hand, and we prayed together. I asked God to please forgive me. I knew I was dying. Something happened inside the truck, but I don't remember exactly if it was before or after we prayed. The radio came on, and I heard a voice saying, *"Only Jesus Christ can take care of you and your problems." I knew right then that I facing death.*

Before this day I had met so many beautiful people who had helped me in many different ways when I was on the road. During my career as a truck driver, I had witnessed strangers risking their lives to help others, like those two people who came to my rescue. Even though they didn't know me, they still took a risk by entering the cab of my truck, which could have caught fire. Disregarding danger, they rushed to help me, a stranger in need.

A fire truck arrived, and they were able to pull the seat back and get me out of the truck. I was in severe pain and having trouble breathing. I remember being inside an ambulance, and I heard someone saying, "Where are we going to do the changes?"

Someone answered, "We are doing the changes here. The patient is suffering from trauma. He has massive internal bleeding. We have the freeway closed so we can treat him right here"

The next thing I remember is waking up inside a helicopter and a lady telling me," Douglas, stay awake! Stay awake! You are going to the best hospital on the West Coast. Have you ever heard of Harbor Trauma Medical Center? We have the best doctors there, and they are going to take care of you." I didn't answer her. I couldn't breathe. I could feel blood coming out of my mouth, nose, and ears.

I felt like I was dying. I saw my entire life flash before my eyes. It was amazing and sad at the same time because I knew I was dying. I had always wondered what it would be like to see my death. And here I was, having that very

experience. Suddenly, I wanted to see my mom and kids to say goodbye to them. I begged God, "Please give me a second chance. Please, don't let me die in this place by myself, I want to see my family one more time."

That day, around the same time when the helicopter was transporting me to the hospital, my girlfriend got a phone call from a gentleman who asked her, "Do you know someone named Douglas?"

"Yes," she told him. "He's my boyfriend. "Who are you, and how did you get my number?"

He told her that he got it from me, but that was not important. He said, "You need to know that he has been in an accident and is being airlifted to a hospital. He is in critical condition, possibly deceased."

Unbelieving, she replied, "This has to be a joke. I just spoke to him over the phone." She thought it had to be a joke, because she had just spoken to me over the phone. She thought it was probably me playing a prank on her.

But the man insisted, "No lady, it's not a joke. A

man identified as Douglas Sandoval was driving a white truck that was involved in a horrible collision. You can contact the emergency line and the hospital in Seattle, and they will give you more information. Still doubtful, she called my mother in California and found out that it was true.

Mom was notified about my accident around the same time. I had made it a habit to call my her every day because she worried about me being out there driving all alone on those busy highways. She always asked me where I was, and I would always tell her, "Mom, even if I tell you where I am, you don't know this place." I always told her anyway, but on May 23, she didn't get a phone call from me.

A state patrol called a friend of mine, Thomas, and told him that I was involved in an accident and to contact my relatives right away because I was in critical condition. He went and told my mother that I had been in an accident. She exclaimed, "You've got to be joking. Please don't play that kind of joke."

"No Sophia," he said, "I'm not joking. I just got a phone call from someone in Seattle. They said Douglas had an accident, and he was airlifted to a hospital. He's in pretty bad shape. They need you right away because someone needs to sign for some surgeries."

Unfortunately, my mother was booked on a flight to Canada by accident. Somehow a clerk had issued her the wrong airline ticket, and she wound up in Canada. This made things more complicated because she needed to be at the hospital ASAP. At first, nobody believed her. When she began crying hysterically, calmed her down enough to understand what had happened and to give her some information about my condition. Finally, she was put on a small airplane and flown back to Seattle. She arrived at hospital the next day at 8:00 a.m.

* * * * *

This was a very difficult time for my mom; she did not want to believe that this had happened to me. She wanted this to be a very bad dream. They gave her the bad news. The doctors told her that they had done everything they could, but there wasn't a big chance for me to come out of it alive. They told her it was going to be a day-by-day progress. My mother and my daughter told me later that they heard the doctor saying that I only had around a fifteen or twenty per cent chance of making it.

While heavily sedated, I saw four young man coming into my room, they took me to these place where two men with no eyes were trying to kill me. At this place there was a big fire. The ground opened and these two men came out of the ground.

One of them pulled out a sword, claiming, "Today you're going to die." At first, I didn't know what was happening. I still had on the same clothes I was wearing when I had the accident, but this place did not look like the place where I had the accident. I remember trying to run from the guy with the sword.

I kept asking, "Am I dead? I think I am dead." I had a horrible sensation in my body, but I wasn't burning or anything like that. I asked God, "Why didn't you give me a second chance?"

Then I heard this voice, behind me. "Douglas, who do you think you are for me to give you a second chance at life if someone else died here the same way you did?"

I asked Him again, "Why didn't you give me a second chance? I asked you to give me at least a chance to see my family."

A few minutes later, I heard the voice repeat, "Douglas, tell me, who do you think you are for me to give you a second chance at life, if someone else died here the same way you did?"

I realized that the voice kept asking the same question over and over. I tried to figure out what God meant when He said," Someone died here the same way you did." I saw a mile marker 7, and the freeway. Then I realized I was looking at the same place where, the day before my truck crashed, another truck driver had been involved in an accident. In fact, some truckers were saying he had died at the scene. At that point I started screaming loudly. I yelled, "Why didn't you give me a second chance?"

A few minutes later I asked the question for the third time. There was no answer. I saw a group of about fifty people holding hands and praying, "Please, God, give Douglas a second chance." Then, I saw the four young man coming back and the two men went back to the ground. Then, the four young men took me back to the hospital.

After having been sedated for almost six days, I woke up and was able to recognize my mother, my children, and some friends, but I struggled to remember what had happened to me. They told me that I had been injured in an accident.

Also, according to the doctors, when I arrived at the hospital, I was conscious and talking, but the only thing I remember from that day was my being transported in a helicopter. According to my kids, when they arrived at the hospital, they were told I was in an induced coma.

This is what the doctors explained to me, they found when I arrived at the hospital on the day of the accident:

1. *Aortic rupture. Aortic dissection.*
2. *Splenic laceration.*
3. *Bilateral pneumothoraxes and hemothoraces.*
4. *Closed right femoral shaft and neck fracture.*
5. *Truamatic arthrotomy of the right knee.*
6. *Right tibia plateau fracture.*
7. *Left rib fractures 6 through 9.*
8. *Splenic infarction.*
9. *Acute respiratory failure.*
10. *Coagulopathy.*

*   *   *   *   *

My left lung was damaged when it collided with my ribs. My right leg was broken into five different parts. I had a laceration of my spleen and several other injuries. According to my doctors, I was very lucky to be alive. Although I was still in serious condition, the critical part had passed.

While reading my medical reports, I learned that something did happen on Friday the twenty-third. And this is how the doctors wrote it on their report.

We therefore elected to proceed to take him back to the Operating Room for exploratory laparotomy to rule out intra-abdominal injury after we established that he had adequately resuscitated from his initial surgery

According to the medical records and from what my mom and my girlfriend told me, something happened on Saturday the twenty-fourth also. My girlfriend told me that when she went to see what was happening, one doctor told her that everything was okay and that they had brought me back. According to my mom, the information she was given by the doctors. There were complications to my lungs and aorta and possible massive loss of blood, but I was out of danger. She noticed that my body was severely swollen. My mother and my girl stated that I was not breathing for almost forty-five minutes.

My daughter Diana reported that one day when she started to translate for my mom, the doctors told her she had to be eighteen or older. I think there was another reason. They knew she was my daughter, and since they were about to tell my mom some bad news, maybe they thought that she was too young to handle it. Mom told the family, after she spoke to the doctors through a translator, that she had to sign a consent form for them to perform another surgery. They also informed her of possibility that I might not make it. This must have been a horrible time for my family.

Now, here is the scary part: My sister told me that she called the company that I worked for and told them that the chances of my coming out alive were almost none. *She also told me that she had notified her employer that she would be taking a week or two off to come to her brother's funeral in Los Angeles. That's how serious my situation was. My relatives and friends had lost hope that I would survive.*

My mom asked me if I remembered the nurse who had come to help me at the time of the accident. Apparently, she had been calling the hospital to check on me. I said I did remember two people coming to my rescue. I wanted to see them both again to just give them a big hug and a *Thank you* for their kindness.

Another someone who showed great concern for me, my mom said, was a nurse at the hospital who came and checked up on me every day. She told my mom to talk to me. She said I could hear her, even if I seemed unconscious. I don't remember hearing her voice, but it did not matter because in her heart she believed I could hear her. Most importantly, *God* heard her prayers.

I was in horrible pain the whole time I was in the hospital. There were times that I would scream so loud that my mom who sat next to me cried in sympathy. She tried to calm me down. She prayed constantly, and she stayed in the hospital with me for the entire time, sleeping in the waiting room on a chair. Sometimes she slipped out and went to a friend's house to take a hurried shower and came back right away.

* * * * *

On June 3, 2003, I remember about six or seven doctors coming into my room. On second thought, I don't know if all of them were doctors, but I could tell by their faces that something was wrong. They came to deliver bad news about something disturbing that showed up in one of the blood tests.

My boss, who was visiting me, was there when they came. My mother was there, also. My mother doesn't speak English, but she didn't need to. They had not said a word yet, but she saw the look on their faces, and she knew something was wrong, she began sobbing before they even said a word. They asked her to leave the room. She refused. She insisted on hearing what they had to say.

They said there was a problem with my spleen. One of the tests showed an infection. They would have to take it out immediately because the infection could travel to the heart or the left lung. They cautioned that it was a very risky operation, but they had no choice. To complicate matters, they couldn't give me any more blood because they had given me too much blood already.

They were going to try to do their best to open me up on one of the same surgeries and remove the spleen. They assured us that they were going to try their best to make sure I wouldn't lose too much blood. I told them, it was okay, that I was happy that I'd seen my family and to do what they had to do.

My mother would not stop crying. I said, "Mom, everything is going to be okay. Just have faith. If God gave me the opportunity to be with you and my kids again, He was not going to let me die during the surgery."

The only person who was not there was my girl-friend. She had gone home to check on the baby. I called her and told her what was about to happen. She was very disappointed that she could not be there for the surgery and to comfort my mom. I told her my boss was there. Mom was not going to be alone. "Just pray," I told her. Then I asked her to put my son on the phone. I wanted to hear his voice one more time.

They wheeled me away to the lab to do some tests to prep for the next day's surgery. I called my kids and assured them that everything was going to be okay and not to worry. I said I loved them very much and to forgive me if I hadn't been a very good father.

That whole night I couldn't sleep. I talked to God, "I know I have seen my kids and my mom and relatives, and I remember what I asked of you when I was in the helicopter, but I know you are a loving God and a gracious God. All I am asking you is to give me one more chance at life! I want to see my kids grow up and finish high school and get married and have kids of their own. I want to hold my grandbabies."

My mom did not sleep that night either. She sat on the chair all night, and my boss stayed with her in the room. I can't imagine what was going through her mind. She had just been through so much the first week, and now she had to sit and wait while I was subjected to another risky surgery.

The next morning a doctor came to see me. She had a smile on her face, I knew she had good news. She said that I was supposed to have died on the operating table. The medical experts couldn't explain how I endured all of the medical traumas that I had suffered. The fact that I am alive today to tell this story is a miracle, a miracle that only God could have accomplished.

She said, "Douglas, we don't know what happened,

but after we did the tests to get you ready for the surgery, we noticed that the infection had disappeared. We don't know how, but it was gone. We are going to do one more test to make sure everything is okay, just for confirmation, but there will be no more surgeries for now. We still have to remove your spleen, but that can be done when you get back to Los Angeles when you're better and have more strength.

When my boss came to see me, about two weeks after the accident, he made a comment after I told him about the voice I heard on the radio. He told me that was impossible because the radio was damaged, and the electrical system was not working because of all the damage to front of the truck.

God listens! He heard me!

I asked, "God, is there anything impossible for you?"

"NOTHING!" "AMEN!"

6

Comeback

I left the hospital on June 10, 2003. When I came to Los Angeles, they took me to USC Medical Center where they performed some more tests. The doctor told me not to worry about my spleen. Even though it was not working, the infection was gone completely. According to the doctor, it had started to shrink, and it would disappear on its own. When I left the hospital about a month later, I had lost almost sixty pounds. I weighed a measly 110 pounds.

At one point, I lost my voice, and that same day I came down with a high fever. I was rushed to hospital, but when I got there, the doctors didn't want to do anything until they got my medical records from Washington. They contacted the hospital at Seattle, but still they couldn't send the paper work right away, so we ended up waiting. Meanwhile, they kept me under observation and monitored the fever. I went to see a throat specialist the next day and he gave me some medication, but for almost two weeks I couldn't speak.

By this time a whole bunch of truck drivers had already come to my house to see me. They were made plans to hold an event at a local park because many more drivers wanted to meet "Caperusita Roja" and "Super Pollo." Approximately 250 truck drivers and their relatives attended that event. Most of them I only knew by their nick names from communicating over the radio, but that day I met them in person. Unfortunately, I could not enjoy the party completely because I was in a wheel chair.

The event was organized by a female truck driver a wonderful friend of mine (her nickname was "Paty Paty), and some other truck drivers. I cried. It was so beautiful to see so many people that I had never met before in person, but over the radio only. Everyone had a story to tell me about how I made them laugh while on the road. I've kept in touch with a few of them over the years. They urged me to go back to truck driving. I told them that I doubted I'd ever go back gain because of my leg, and even if I could, I could never again put my mom through the torture of worrying.

They all had tags, so I could read their names, but at the end of the day, I had shaken hands with everybody. Among the crowd, I saw a guy with a long hair who I recognized right away. It was Renegado. With him was his wife, the lady who had cursed me out one day long ago. Renegado told her, "Okay, go ahead. You said when you met Caperusita, you were going to beat the heck out her for messing around with men on that road. Now is your chance. There she is, in a wheel chair, I don't think she can't fight back."

A few days after that event, the couple came to visit me. She told me that she was under the impression that I was a real woman, and she apologized for cursing at me. I told her, "Don't worry. You were not the only one who had cursed the heck out of me on the road."

All these drivers who came that day, and many others, were the ones, whose lives I had touched with my jokes. My family and friends were amazed to see so many truck drivers and their wives and kids at that event. My family knew that I was crazy and used to be a joker, but they did not know that I had so many friends. There were even people from other states who came to my celebration.

People who happened to be visiting the park that day came to ask what was happening. Once they learned about the purpose of the celebration, they came to shake my hand and to hear how I had survived my accident.

For the first three months after I came from the hospital, my mom would sleep most of the time next to my bed, or she slept on a sofa in the living room with the door to the bedroom open. I had this weight wrapped around my leg to hold it in place in order for me to get some sleep. Because it was very uncomfortable, I would remove it. My mom stayed next to the bed in case I fell.

Whenever I had to use the bathroom, she carried me to the bathroom and helped me to shower and/or use the facilities.

She helped me get in and out of bed. She pushed my wheel chair when I went for my doctor appointments, or if I wanted to outside to get some air. She got up in the morning to prepare breakfast. So, I could take my medications, she helped me put on my underwear, pants and socks because I could not bend my body. For those three months, I was her baby, a newborn, at that. Sometimes at night I could feel her next to my bed, making sure I was okay and that my leg was in the right position. My mother was my nurse for many months. She became an expert on my medications, and she made sure that I took them on time. She would always have clean clothes next to my bed ready for the next day before I went to bed.

*   *   *   *   *

At this crucial time of my life, God had provided me an angel to take care of me, in the form of my mother. She was my greatest motivation for recovering. Sometimes she gazed at me and asked gently, "Are you okay, son? Do you need something?"

I would just as gently remind her, "Mom, you just asked me that a few minutes ago." It was not easy even for her to go to the store to get groceries because she did not want to leave me alone at the house. This tragedy provided my mom an opportunity to take care of her baby boy again.

Even though family and friends, fellow truck drivers, and even complete strangers, had celebrated my recovery, I was still not out of the woods. At one point I was having breathing problems. The doctors had given me a machine to help me breathe, but I still found it difficult to breathe. The condition lasted so long I was afraid that I was going to die in my sleep. My mother, of course, refused to leave my bed side at night. She only relented during the times when two of my friends would come and stay with me so she could get some rest.

One day a pastor, by the name of Rigoberto Marin, came to my house with some of the members of his church. I will never forget that day. He came to my bed and put his hands on my chest. As soon as he lay his hands on me, I felt my lungs move and air rush through my lungs. What a beautiful sensation! I breathed on my own, but I still followed the doctor's orders and kept using the machine. When I went to see the doctor, I told him what had happened. He was excited to hear that I was breathing normally again,

but he advised me to keep using the machine at night in case I began to feel any shortness of breath.

As if breathing problems were not enough, for almost a month I had a pain in my foot. The pain was so severe that, one night after seeing my mom sleeping in a chair next to the bed, I told God that if I was going to die of this pain, it would have been better for me to die at the hospital or during the accident. The pain was so agonizing that I could not sleep at all. And I just could not stand to see my mother suffer such worry about me anymore. I suspected that she was suffering from depression, but she kept up a strong front for me. She tried not to show it, but I could see it. She was not eating, and sometimes she cried a lot. Despite her anxiety, she seemed happy that I was still alive after all I had been through.

*   *   *   *   *

I had been injecting myself with blood thinners every day for almost two months. I had stuck the needle so many places on my stomach, I ran out of room. When I told one of my doctors about it, he gave me pills instead.

I never will never forget when I first met my primary doctor, Robert Audell.

He asked me if any of the other doctors had told me that I was supposed to have died in that accident, I said, yes. He was an orthopedic doctor, but I wanted him to be my primary doctor, because from the moment I met him, he said something that got my attention. He told me it was going to be an honor for him to take care of me because I was a miracle. He marveled that I had survived the accident to him it was beyond belief.

A few months after I had met him, I showed him a picture of how I looked before the accident, He was impressed. But I said, "Wait, Doctor. I did not show you the picture just to show off. Since you have worked with professional athletes, I want to know if I can ever look like this again? Can I get back in shape again?"

He repeated almost the same thing other doctors had told me. "Douglas, you should be thankful that you are alive. Forger about your muscle. You still have *you*. And, Douglas, you still have a long recovery, so get that out of your mind for the next few years. You look like a guy with great spirit, so I think you will be able to do it eventually, but I don't think you can start right now. Of course, he laughed when he said that because I was in a wheel chair, and I couldn't even walk without crutches, let alone work out.

A few months after I came from the hospital, a truck driver, friend of mine, called me and asked if I knew that something was going to happen to me on that trip. I told him that I had this weird feeling a week before the accident and that it had worried me until that day of the accident. He exclaimed, "Hey, Pollito, I believe you. I believe you, Pollito."

He sounded strange. "Is everything okay?" I asked.

He answered, "Pollito, guess what I have in my truck, I got your QUALCOMM that you had on your truck on your last trip. Guess what I just read. I read the message you sent to your dispatcher, where you told him, you were scared and that you had witnessed an accident in Fresno of a set of doubles."

I told him that I had totally forgotten about that message. This conversation gave me more motivation not to give up, and at the same time I wondered. Was I supposed to die that week? I remember the notes I wrote to my kids, telling them goodbye. Ironically, during the months before the accident, I felt like I was on top of the world. I wanted to become a professional body builder. I had everything I wanted at that moment. I wasn't thinking about dying.

I don't know which doctor a made this comment, since I had so many doctors. but I was asked if I had any thoughts of suicide. I told him that one night, after so much pain and after seeing my mother suffering so much, I told God in one of my prayers that it would have been better for me to die in the accident or the hospital. Because of this comment I was sent to a psychologist.

When I met Mr. Hirsh for the first time, he was also surprised that I was sitting in front of him. He asked why I had made those comments and if I had any thought of committing suicide. I told him that sometimes I would go to sleep and did not want to wake up, but it was not like I wanted to kill myself. I told him a few times that I was afraid about my future. I did not know if I was going to be normal again, if I was going to able to run and jump and do normal things. What kind of job I was going to be able to perform and if I was going to ever work again? I told him that it freaked me out to think that I had plastic wrapped around my main vein and that my spleen was disappearing and that I had all these screws and metal in my right leg. Additionally, there were many were other issues affecting my health.

* * * * *

Finally, the time came for me to learn how to walk again. I knew this was not going to be easy. For the first two weeks, I had to learn how to walk again, step by step. It was very depressing having to let someone hold me from the back with a strap to make sure I didn't fall. After two weeks of going to a professional therapist, I realized that I would have to do this on my own, too. So, I started doing therapy at home. I used anything I could find around the house. I exercised my leg. All those years of training and working out paid off. After a month, I was already walking a little bit without the crutches.

One of the guys at the place where I went for therapy asked me if I was doing anything on my own, I said, yes. He told me to be careful, not to get hurt. When I went back next time, I showed him a picture of how

I looked before the accident. He was impressed. "You got this, Douglas," he assured me. "You are not going to need a lot of therapy. You can do this on your own." The first three months after I started therapy were extremely exhausting. There were moments when I did not feel it like going to therapy or even working out at the house. Then I would remember my mom's anguish about my suffering and look at pictures of my healthier days. That was my motivation.

By December I was not using the crutches as much and using the cane more. I kept telling myself, "I am not going just to sit around and just wait to get better." Also, by this time I had moved to another facility with a gym so I could use the pool; that helped me a lot.

By the end of 2003, my father got a visa and came to visit me. I was so excited to see him again. I told him that he almost missed seeing me forever.

While he was here, he visited me a few times.

By January of 2004, I started driving myself to therapy. I was also helping my mom more. I took her to the grocery store, and she went with me to my doctor appointments. During this period, my girlfriend came to spend time with me. It was our son Matthew's birthday, and we threw him a party at my house. She stayed for a few days, but she had to go back home. Before she left, we made plans for her to come back by March so we could get married.

In January 2004, things took a turn for the worse. A van cut in front of me as I drove home from my therapy session. I hit the van in the front. The impact was so severe that the engine from my car almost felt off. This was incredible! Why was this happening to me? Please, not now, not when I was starting to get around by myself!

I called my mother, "Mom, I am going to tell you something, but please don't freak out because I am okay, but I just had another accident."

The first question that came out of her mouth was "Is your heart okay?"

"Yes," I lied. "I'm fine." Actually, I was having some chest pains. When the ambulance arrived, the attendant asked me to hang up the phone. I told him I needed to know where they were taking me so I could tell my mom.

I told her where they were taking me. Then I said, "Just don't panic. If the situation was bad, I wouldn't be talking to you right now." She did not want to hang up. She kept asking, "Why is this happening to you?" I told her I had to hang up and not to worry, just get to the hospital.

I told the paramedics about my major accident. When they examined me and saw the scars from my surgeries, they rushed me to the hospital. I told them that I was having chest pains, and I could also feel the screws in my knees. It felt like they had moved or something. They took some X-rays. They said they could see a tiny fracture in my chest and some broken bones in my knee. That was not good news.

My mom and a few relatives arrived shortly after I was admitted. I did not tell her about the chest fracture. I only told her about my knee. They kept me there for a while and did some more tests and then they sent me home.

The next day I went see my primary doctor. At first, he was worried, but after some more X-rays, it turned out that nothing serious had happened. The doctor joked, "Are you trying to kill yourself? Because there are other ways you can do this?" Of course, we laughed.

I came back with a joke of my own. "Nope, it's just that with the first accident, I only fractured the left ribs. I wanted to fracture the right ribs this time, so there would be a balance, but I missed the target and hit the center. Those damn airbags actually work!"

We all laughed, but this accident was about to put me way back in my schedule for rehab, and I was in a hurry to get back to a normal life. For now, though, I had to wait. For almost three months, I suffered with horrible pains in my chest and knee. I had to do more therapy, and it felt like it was never going to end. I had to use the crutches again and a walker. I could not bend my knees for a while, and I began using a knee brace. Once again, I went through some sleepless nights, and once again my mom had to watch over me to make sure I slept comfortably in bed.

* * * * *

In March 2004, my girlfriend and my baby Mathew came home to stay. Finally, Mom had some help. We decided to move to another place. We also got married the same month. By the end of the year we moved to the house next door to my mom's house.

This worked better for all us. My wife did not have to worry about me and Matthew now that she had help with my mom right next door. And my mother could keep an eye on me without having to give up her rest all of the time.

This same year my son Douglas came back to live with me. I had a big conversation with him. The first thing I told him was: "Son, you do know that I have full custody of you, so this is what is going to happen. Your mother keeps telling me to send you back almost every year. So. Guess what? No more! I had been doing that because she loves you, but every time you went back to her, she kept sending you back to me. This is hurting you, and it's hurting me and your mother. But most of all, you're hurting yourself. You are about to start high school. That was your last time living with your mom. You will not leave this house until you graduate from high school. And mark my words. You will graduate. I will make sure of that.

"If you think that you are going to convince your mother to let you come back, forget about it. I have full custody of you, and even if your mom decided to fight me in court, she would lose. Also, I will be at every meeting or parents' counseling at school, and if you get any D's or F's, you will go to summer school every summer.

"I will be your shadow, and I will be watching all the time. I have all the time in the world because I am not working. Furthermore, you will walk to school. I will buy you a bike, in case you want to ride it to school sometimes, but if it gets stolen, you will walk. I will only drive you to school when is raining. By the time you are done, you will have muscles in your legs, bigger than the ones I used to have." To his credit, Douglas, Jr. went to school every summer to make up any lapses in his grades. Not only did he graduate, he got an award for excellent attendance.

In November 2004, I was having some low back pain. And when I say pain, I mean *pain*! I could not even sit on the toilet without help. They did a MRI and they noticed that the L5-S1 disc were open 6-mm

The doctor told me that surgery might be necessary. I asked him if there was anything else that we could do beside surgery because I was very scared to have back surgery. He told me the other option was for me to do more therapy. He sent me to do more therapy. A beautiful Asian lady told me, "If you don't want to have surgery, you will have to do exactly what I tell you. If you don't follow my instructions, you will be wasting your time. Then, they will have to open you lower back. You've already had major surgery on your upper back and having another one is no good. "

I guess that her strict tone was her method to motivate me, and I thank God because it worked. For the next seven months it was horrible. My son and my wife had to help me around the house. Even when I had to use the toilet, they helped me. The pain was so intense that I needed help just to sit down on the sofa, but I was determined not to have back surgery. I had to get help just to walk down the steps at the house, and there were only two steps. The owner of the house, Mr. Miguel, was so nice that he made adjustments in the interior to enable me to move around inside and outside of the house.

I did therapy at a gym facility. Sometimes when I did therapy at my house, I followed my therapist's instructions. I was taking pain medication, but it was not helping. For a moment I thought about telling the doctor to go ahead with the back surgery, but I gave up that idea. I had to keep trying. Some people told me that was a bad idea, and that I should not do this on my own, they urged me to let the doctors cut into my back.

By August of 2005, I was feeling better, but I still suffered significant pain.

In September of 2005, I had another MRI, which showed that there was some improvement, so my doctor decided to give me an injection to help me with the pain. Unfortunately, it did not help much, maybe for a few weeks.

For a while instead of going to therapy for my lower back, I did it at my house. My doctor told me the day that he got the MRI results that he had never met a person like me before, with such a great spirit. He was amazed that I had such strength and determination after all I been through. He told me people usually give up after having such a difficult time, but I was exceptional. I was fighting. He said some patients decide to go ahead and have surgery to avoid the tedious, painful therapy. He was surprised that I stopped coming to therapy and continued with working alone at home. He found it remarkable that I was able to fix my spine without having to undergo surgery. I remember making a joke and telling him, "I must not be very good for business."

He said something in reply that I still remember this day. "Douglas, I wish I had more patients like you. When I first met you, you came in a wheel chair. You looked very skinny, but look at you now. You look better than me and some of the guys here." I was still using my cane, and he said, "I wouldn't be surprised if you stopped using the cane pretty soon."

I promised him, "I definitely will!"

* * * * *

One day while walking down some stairs, I felt something unusual in my hip, a strange kind of pain. After having some X-rays done, my doctor told me that one of the screws in my hip had migrated very close to the upper bone. He decided to remove the rod that was inside my femur and also remove some screws. He performed the procedure in 2005.

Once gain my mom and my wife had to stand night watch. The doctor told me that he was going to try to finish in less than four hours to avoid any complications. My mom and my wife were nervous. I told them to stop being nervous, that this was just a walk on the park for me, compared to what I went through when the accident happened. I did not want to tell them that I was freaking out. When they took me to the operation room, I told them, "I will be right back in four hours. Fix me some chicken soup. "

Mom had mention that she was not feeling well. She was feeling tired for no reason sometimes. Then it happened. I was at church when I got a phone call that my mother had suffered a heart attack. I rushed to the hospital. When I got there, I was told she was a delicate condition. They were running some tests. and when they got the results, they would tell exactly what was wrong. They told me the attack was caused by too much stress. Her blood pressure was dangerously high. I told them that what she had gone through with me over the years most likely had undoubtedly stressed her out. The doctor's final diagnosis was she needed to rest as much as possible and avoid all worries.

I felt like her condition was my fault because she had gone through so much in the last three years that her body and heart could not take it anymore.

After her heart attack, my mom was never the same.

In 2006, I told my doctor that I was going to start working out and lifting weights again, but I was going to be careful. I told him that I missed my muscles. I was going to try to get them back. He told me be careful and not to forget that I still had some metal and screws in my right leg.

When I started working out, it felt good to do something that had helped me out in the past to deal with my problems. Now participating in physical activity was going to help me get through this latest crisis. I got a gym member ship, and I went for a while, but then I bought me some exercise equipment. From then on, I only went to the gym to use the swimming pool. I worked out at my house, and about one year later, I had a great upper body and had gone from 130 to 150 pounds.

When I went to court, the attorney for the insurance company said, "You look amazing. Look at you now. About a year ago, you looked like a stick. I am jealous of you. You look better than I do, and after all you've been through. My attorney told me that it will be a good idea to wear a long sleeve shirt when I came

to court. I agreed but it's not like I was faking my injuries. Also, I was about to have another surgery to remove the last of the metal still in my body. Building up my body was going to help me to be mentally prepared and strong by then.

I saw a lot of people in court who looked depressed. I heard people crying in pain. One time, I asked a guy what had happened to him. He told me that he had been injured on the job, and he had been fighting his case for a while. I asked him what happened to him. He told me that he had fallen and hurt his back. He wanted to know what I was there for. I showed him the some of the scars from my surgeries. When I told him, it had been about six years since my accident, he was amazed, "You look really good, like you work out a lot. You don't look like you've been in an accident at all. Isn't that going to be an issue for your case?"

"You see all these people here?" I replied. "I bet you some of them probably sit all day in their houses just watching TV and doing nothing. They go do their therapy and don't try to do any exercise at home to take care of themselves. You know why? Because they think the worse they look, the more money they will get."

"I continued, "It is not about money. Yes, I understand the insurance is intended to take care of you in case something happens. That is why you pay for it. But I still have a long way to go, and when this case is settled, I want to be ready to go back to work or be prepared for whatever life brings."

Several people suggested that I should be a personal trainer for others who have been the victims of accidents. In my opinion, they needed more help with their mental issues than they did with physical problems.

* * * * *

In 2007, I had surgery to clear out the last of the metal and screws. I was excited to finally get rid of all that metal in my body.

Having survived all of this, I was invited to a church to give my testimony. When I finished, the pastor approached and asked me if I could hold some classes. He said that I was "an inspiration!" For six months. I taught a class once a week. I also went to a

Bible institute for a few years. After I finished my classes as a student, I was asked to become one of the teachers at the institute. I taught two years at the Institute.

By September of 2008, I was discharged from therapy and given a green light to go back to work. Finally, after almost six years of rehab, two surgeries, many months of therapy, multiple appointments to different doctors, and sometimes too much pain medication, I was now ready in some ways to go back to my normal life.

I don't think I would have made it through all those years, if I was not mentally and physically prepared. Most of all, my faith in God, my family and friends who were there for me when I needed them most, sustained me. Almost six years later as I returned to an almost normal life, I was scared and excited.

Not all doctors had given me good news when I was on disability, but no matter what they told me, whether it was good or bad, I was already mentally prepared. If they said I had to do two months of therapy, I did four. It wasn't a matter of not following their instructions. I just needed to do more on my own.

* * * * *

I had no idea what I was going do for employment. I could not stand, sit, or walk for a long time. What could I do? Luckily, one day, a friend told me that his boss was hiring guards. I made an appointment and went to meet him. This guy was an amazing person from the beginning. I told him my situation, and I explained to him the things I could not do, He told me not worry about it and that he would make sure to send me to places where I would be able to sit and stand whenever I needed to. It was not easy at first to accommodate my new life style. I had not worked for almost six years. Sometimes my right leg hurt a lot, but I kept at it. My boss constantly asked me if I was okay and to always let him know if I needed anything.

In 2009, my wife and I decided to have another baby, and Janet was born in December 16, 2009. That same year my boss got a new account with a gated community. "Briarwood Community Center," located in Inglewood, California. This place would change my life in some way. My son Douglas graduated from high school soon after I got the job, and he started working as a security guard along with me. At this place I could sit down and stand up and walk whenever I wanted to.

This was an ideal job for me. My prayers had been answered. It was just seven minutes away from house, and my boss made it possible for me to have a shift to accommodate my personal life. I met some wonderful people at the new job. In two years of working there, I already knew almost everybody. People always asked me how was it possible that I knew everybody's names, including some of people who were just guests rather than residents. I told them that I had been involved in a terrible accident, and I was given a second chance at life. To make sure that I would succeed, God had made me better than I was before the accident. My wife and I, started having some problems, we were continuously fighting.

By January, 2013, my wife and I separated. I fought for four years to keep our marriage from falling apart, but at one point it was too much. I just could not handle the pressure. We are still friends, and we both take good care of our children. We have two amazing kids. My ex-wife always wanted a boy and a girl. We are the parents of Matthew and Janet. I love them, and they sure keep their dad going.

We filed for divorce, and in June of 2014, we sold our house. The second time around, my life might have changed for the worse; except this time, I did the opposite of what I had done during my first marriage. I got closer to God, and once again my faith brought me through another crisis.

I am fifty years old, and I have a good life. I have God, a good job, some wonderful children, seven grandchildren.

Diana, Hellen and Josh, live in Tacoma, Washington.

Diana has two beautiful kids, Jayden and Bellen.

Hellen has two beautiful girls, Yolandita and Marley.

Josh has a son name, Ezra.

My son Douglas lives in Los Angeles, and he has two beautiful girls, Nicole and Genesis. I see them almost every weekend.

My son Alex lives with his mom in Los Angeles. He doesn't have any children.

I try to go and visit my kids almost every year in Washington.

Recently, I met a wonderful lady, thanks to Morena, my cousin. She announced, "I found the woman you are going to spend the rest of your life with." I went out on a first date with my future wife Vicky. After we dated for a while, we did decide to get married. God willing, we will live happily ever after!

7

Faith Wins Out

After this accident, my faith would never be the same. I was already a man of faith, but now my faith had increased. I used to listen to other people's testimony about what God had done for them. I believed them, and I used to give God the glory, but now I had my own experience. I will never forget the doctors' expressions when they told me that they had to remove my spleen and warned me about the possible complications. At that moment, I thought if God brought me out of that truck alive and kept me from dying while I was in critical condition, he would certainly bring me out of that operating room safely.

I woke up in the hospital after being in critical condition for a few days, and seeing my family there, I remembered what I had asked of God, when I was in the helicopter. My prayers had been answered. Although I knew I was not out of the woods yet, I knew that I was going to be okay, in spite of my brush with death.

I had been running from God for almost ten years, but now I had experienced His love for me. Being surrounded by my family in the hospital, strengthened my belief that I would emerge victorious from this trial. I knew that God had given me another chance at life. My faith grew; it went from I believe in God, to I know He can do anything!

When I heard the doctors saying, "We don't know how you survived all the time without medical attention." When I heard them saying, "You were supposed to die from the impact." When I heard them saying, *"You were supposed to bleed to death, just minutes after the accident."* When I heard them making all of those pronouncements, I was hearing, "Only God could have done this." That is how I knew my faith had grown stronger.

I knew my recovery was not going to be easy, I had a long journey ahead of me, but I had survived the worse part. When my son Douglas came back, my mom and wife were worried that he would interfere with my rehabilitation. Instead, having him with me was great motivation. I knew he needed me. He had been through so much in the last seven years, moving back and forth between separate parents and his grandfather. I did not see his presence as an obstacle, I saw it as an opportunity keep me active while I was taking care of him. Beside I needed more people to help me get around, and who could do it better than my son?

Now more than ever, I needed to get better sooner. What others saw as an obstacle, I saw as an opportunity to help myself. It was about time that I started talking to myself and being convinced that I would recover and stop entertaining negative thoughts. After all, I had a family who needed me, and I had no intentions to let them down. Thus, I had to reprogram myself, and faith would play a big part.

I had to feel positive about my future. My mother needed me. She had done her part. Now it was my turn to help her. I couldn't let her down. I couldn't let my kids down. Nor could I let the rest of my family down.

Anyone can say, "You be will be ok, don't worry about it, but it takes faith to believe that everything will be all right, but you also have to believe in yourself. When the doctor told me that he might have to do operate on my lower back, it was faith that made me believe that I could fix the problem without surgery. I don't think I could have withstood the intense pain I suffered without faith in myself and the belief that God would take care of me. I don't think my mom could have stood by me so long and so strong without faith.

* * * * *

When I left my home during the third week of May 2003, I left in one piece, walking by myself. Who would have thought that a month later, I was going to be coming back to my mom's home in a wheel chair? I used to have my own place, but now I had to stay with my mom because I couldn't take care of my myself.

I had to move from my apartment and sell all my belongings because they would not fit in my mother's place. I had just bought everything six months before, and now I had to practically give everything away.

On top of everything else, my dream of becoming a bodybuilder was gone. My dream of growing old driving a truck was gone, also. So many dreams, so many plans, so few chances. All gone.

In a brief moment, my life took another turn. It took me a while to realize the magnitude of what had happened to me. But later, I realized that all those things that I thought I wasn't going to be able to do were just part of my past.

I was about start a new chapter in life. I was about to embark on a fresh journey. I knew my life was not going to be the same, and I was scared at first. I did not know what the future would bring.

I talked to myself. *What are you going to do now? Look at you. You are not the same person anymore. You are not the same person that left this place.* It was true that a totally different person had come and taken my place. When I looked in the mirror, I saw a different person. For a while I sank into depression. I wanted those months to go by quickly. I was impatient to start therapy. I wanted to walk again. That person in that

wheel chair was not the same guy who had left a few
months before.

Some days I did not eat at all, I didn't want to take
the pain medication. I stayed in bed all day. My mom
would try anything to cheer me up, to keep me moti-
vated, by telling me that I used to be a strong person
and not to give up and to think about my kids and that
they still needed me, and that one day I was going to
be normal again.

I hated to see myself in that wheelchair. I wanted
to just get up and grab it and throw it outside and never
see it again. When I started walking on crutches and
moving around on my own, I realized that everything
was not lost. I started to see life differently. I started
going to church more. I knew my life was never going
to be the same, so I had to adapt to the new life style.
The first year was the worst one, because of the second accident that I had, but I did not let that bring me
down. I was not the only one who had to adapt to my
new lifestyle. The lives of the people around me—my
family, my closest friends—were also affected. By ne-
cessity, my lifestyle became their lifestyle because they
were my main support.

* * * * *

My mom went through so much from the moment she heard about my accident and those seven
hours while she was in Canada. All she could do was
cry and cry while she begged them to call Seattle because her son was dying in a hospital and she wanted
to see him. My mom would never be the same after
suffering through this crisis with me. She went many
nights without sleeping. For days she would go without eating because she had lost her appetite. She lost
too much weight. Sometimes I saw her cry for no ap-
parent reason. When I asked her why she was crying,
she would respond, "I am crying with happiness because you are here with us." But I knew she was lying. She was crying because the stress was crushing
her. Despite her constant sadness, she always found a
way to pull through the bad times. She was (and is) an
amazing person.

Some of my kids were too young to understand
what was happening, except for my daughter Diana
and my son Josh. Diana told me that she went into depression. She did not want to believe that it was her

father on that bed in that hospital. She did not want to go back with her mom to her home. She wanted to stay there with grandma at the hospital to be close to her dad. She wanted to be involved in the decisions her grandma was making when I was in critical condition. When Diana was born, I wanted a boy, but when I first saw her eyes wide open looking at me, I totally forgot about wishing for a boy. I fell in love with my darling daughter and those eyes and thirty years later, I still love them.

Even though we were not together at that time, my ex-girlfriend Monica was there at the hospital most of the time. Me and her were making plans to get married and to work things out in our relationship, and hour later, I was fighting to stay alive? We had just spoken on the phone that day, and hours later she did not know whether I was going to live or die.

When she made the decision to get back with me, she knew I was not the same person she had dated before, that big man with muscles, who thought that he was unstoppable. Now her "new" boyfriend weighed about110 pounds and nobody knew how long his recovery was going to be.

When I was in the hospital, I thought I was not going to leave there alive. For a moment I felt this would be my last stop. But those who cared—family and friends, fellow truckers—encouraged me. "Douglas, be strong and don't give up hope. Just have faith in God. Believe that you can pull through this."

Those three weeks in the hospital helped me realize so many things. I began seeing life in a different way. I vowed to my family that if I came out of this alive, I would never take life for granted. There were nights that I would go to sleep, and I thought that I was not going to wake up.

When I finally left the hospital, I was so excited that I was coming home; I knew the recovery was going to take a long, long time. I knew I was embarking on an uphill battle. I had to have a plan, and at the end of the plan, there was advice:

I told myself. If I can overcome this adversity, I can do anything. I would be able to function normally again. I knew there would be moments when I would want to give up, but I was determined to keep on "keeping on."

Going back to church and being active helped me

to persist through all those painful years of therapy. Another source of comfort was meeting people who hugged me every day, who were strangers, but who seemed like people I had known for a long time. Love has an amazing effect in adverse situations. People kept coming to my house just to see how I was doing and to spend time with me. No medicine in the world can replace that kind of love and attention.

I once met with a cardiologist for an evaluation. I will never forget that day. Even though he had my files in his hands, he asked me who I was. I told him my name, and he asked, "Are you the guy from these files?"

"Yes, it said Douglas Sandoval, right?

He looked at me and asked for my birth date, where the accident happened, and a whole bunch of other questions.

Then he said, "This is impossible. There is no way someone could have survived with a ruptured aorta for that long. If I am not mistaken, you had the first surgery to repair your aorta, almost an hour after the accident, but you also had other problems when you arrived at the hospital. You are a miracle! You were supposed to die just minutes after the accident or immediately from the impact.

"Tell me, do you believe in God? Do you go to church?"

"Yes," I responded, wondering about the reason for these questions.

"Then find a church that is open every day. You are a miracle walking! I have been a doctor for more than forty years, and I've seen cases similar to yours, but your case is unique. You should have died that day. You should be thankful to the doctors who operated on you. They did a phenomenal job of putting you back together!"

He then called a few of his colleagues and raved about me. One of then asked if he was sure I was the person who was named in the files. Whenever I've met people like this doctor, I feel powerful. I believe that I can do anything. Here were people who had dedicated their lives to helping people, and they believed that I was special. When I left his office that day, I was transformed. I began to think that people who admired me were put in my life for a reason. The doctor had said he was excited to meet me. When he read my file before he arrived at the examination room, he said he expected to see someone in a depressed mode, but when he saw me, he thought I was a patient who was placed in his exam room by mistake. Just like every other doctor I met, he told me that I had a long journey ahead. He said that he was going to tell all of his colleagues and friends that he had met me. His words stuck in my mind with me for a while.

It is important to understand that our minds retain volumes of thought, including those positive comments; our minds can be so powerful. The body has limitations, but not the brain. The brain is an amazing organ. My body used to tell me, "I am done. I can't do this no more," but my brain rejected that thought. My mind resisted; it said, NO!" My mind used to tell my legs, "Just a few more steps," while my body protested, "No, I'm done. Let's go home."

While on a visit to the Department of Motor Vehicles, I saw a man on crutches, not regular crutches, but crutches for special needs and he had very small legs. He pushed himself up to sit on a chair. He was an employee, despite his disability; he seemed to be enjoying his job. Looking at him that day, I told myself. I have to get back on my feet. I have to get back in shape. The metal and screws in my legs are not going to stop me from doing the things I want to do.

* * * * *

One day I felt dizzy, and I had a strong headache. The doctors ran some tests and discovered that my cholesterol was super high. They were going to put me on medication, but I said, "No, I don't need it. I know what I need to do.

"But your pressure is too high," they said. "We need to bring it down right away."

Again, I refused, "Just give me six months and if is not down by then, I will take the medication." I changed my diet and started to do a lot of cardio, but I also educated myself on how to manage this type of illness. Six months later, my blood pressure was normal. The doctor said I was incredible. He hadn't believed that I could do it. It is now fifteen years later. I have not taken any medication for my cholesterol, and it remains at an almost normal level.

I once met a gentleman at a place where I went to give my testimony. He had broken his tibia and had been on crutches for a while. He was inspired by my testimony and wanted to hear more about me. He wanted to know how I had "done it." I told him, "God had given me the strength, but I also knew that I had to do my part. There were moments at the beginning when I did not know what I was going to do, but I never gave up."

At another church, another brother approached me and told me that everything that I had said that night was meant especially for him. According to him, he was the reason I happened to be there that night. He was having some problems with his health, and even though my testimony was not about health issues, he said that he was touched by the fact that I did not give up and most importantly, I kept my faith. I sat with him for a while, and I told him that there were many times when I had the feeling that I was not going to pull through it, but I always have found something to motivate me. This was the message I gave to him that night. It's a message that I've given to others who have asked me for a message of hope when they, like I did, hit the inevitable rough spots on the highways our lives.

Conclusion

Triumph

When I was a kid, my life was beautiful. I don't remember ever getting sick, I don't remember ever being sad. I was poor, but I was a happy, poor kid.

I did not know there were other countries beside the one we lived in. I didn't even know there were more states in my country. We had no TV. All we had were friends and family.

The war in El Salvador marked a time of great tragedy and change in the country. It marked an even greater change for me. When the war started, I did not know what a war was. When my mom left us to go to America, I was sad and angry because she left us, but when I finally learned the reason she had gone, I was mad, mad at the people responsible on both sides, those for and against the war. I was not the only child whose parents had to leave their countries to look for a better or safer life but being without my mother was not easy. Yes, even though we had our grandma with us, it was not the same.

Coming to America was one the most beautiful experiences I ever had. This country welcomed me and my family with open arms. At first it was hard to adapt to a completely different environment. However, I was very happy to be in a country so different from mine. Everything was bigger and better here. The best fast food restaurants, movie theaters. The best amusement parks, the best TV shows. I watched cartoons all day when I was not in school or playing. Even though I enjoyed living here, I was not completely happy. I missed my grandma and my sister, my friends. I missed everybody. I would cry because I kept thinking I would never see them again. Sometimes I wonder if this fear played a part in wanting so desperately to be surrounded by my loved ones when my life changed.

Just when I thought everything was over, God came into my life. I got married and started a family. Everything was fine for a while. I had a wonderful life. I had a job. I was an active member of a church. I had everything I wanted and needed. The most beautiful experience ever was when I saw my first child. I was in love with this little girl. And when my other kids were born, my joy knew no bounds.

But, then one day, misfortune struck and my life took another turn. I lost my wife. My children were no longer with me. I was devastated. I thought I was not going to be able to weather the storm. I was afraid I'd go back to the old me. I tried different things to dealt with the separation from my family, and for a while I thought I had been successful. Working out helped me out in some ways to deal with my depression. It helped me forger for a while, but it was not enough, that's why I became a trucker.

I wasn't running from the responsibility of being a father. On the

contrary, when I was driving, and if I had a chance, I applied for trips going through the area where my kids lived in order to stop and visit with them. Becoming a trucker was one of the most beautiful and unforgettable accomplishments of my life. I experienced my greatest thrills traveling the highways and getting to know this amazing country.

I was a part of a group of people who helped move the economy (merchandise) of this country. More importantly, I met many interesting, wonderful people during my travels. I enjoyed every single minute that I was out there. If I could do it again, I would not think twice. I'd gladly climb aboard one of those trucks and drive again. One of my biggest dreams is to stop and meet people and see things in every state.

There is no doubt that my faith in my family and God played an immeasurable part in my rehabilitation and in my life in general. Sometimes I just wanted to give up and just let time go by, but inside of my head, I heard a voice that encouraged me, "Keep on trucking! Don't give up, don't give up, you can do this!"

This has been my mantra through the best and worst of times in my life. Remember to enjoy life and the people around you. Another is: Never stop living your dreams. You don't know when death will be come knocking on your door. Most of all, be in peace with God and life. When you are, life will always be a comeback.

Bibliography

Ching, Erik, *Stories of Civil War in El Salvador: A Battle over Memory*, (University of North Carolina Press: Chapel Hill, N.C., 2016).

Coutin, Susan Bibler, *Exiled Home: Salvadoran Transnational Youth in the Aftermath of Violence (Global Insecurities)*, (Duke University Press Books: Durham, N.C., 2016).

Duffin, Jacalyn, *Medical Miracles: Doctors, Saints, and Healing in the Modern World* (Oxford University Press: New York, 2008).

Gorkin, Michael, *From Grandmother to Granddaughter: Salvadoran Women's Stories*, (University of California Press: Berkeley, 2000).

Gupta, Sanjay, *Cheating Death: The Doctors and*

Medical Miracles that Are Saving Lives Against All Odds, (Grand Central Life & Style: New York, 2010).

Lesslie, Robert D., *Miracles in the ER: Extraordinary Stories from a Doctor's Journal* (Harvest House Publishers: Eugene, Ore., 2014).

McPhee, Andy, *Medical Miracles*, (Scholastic: New York, 2010).

Moodie, Ellen, *El Salvador in the Aftermath of Peace: Crime, Uncertainty, and the Transition to Democracy (The Ethnography of Political Violence)*, (University of Pennsylvania Press: Philadelphia, Penn., 2012).

Rock Russell, Brent, *Miracles & Mayhem in the ER: Unbelievable True Stories from an Emergency Room Doctor*, (Russell Media: Boise, Id., 2013).

Wadkins, H. Timothy, *The Rise of Pentecostalism in Modern El Salvador: From the Blood of the Martyrs to the Baptism of the Spirit (Studies in World Christianity)* (Baylor University Press: Waco, Tex., 2017).

Index

About the Author

For the last 10 years I have been trying to write a book about my near death experience. Well, finally it is here!

I have seven wonderful children and seven amazing grandbabies. I work as the Security Post Commander at a wonderful gated community located Inglewood California (Briarwood Community Center).

I still work out, but not like I used too because of the many broken bones and low back problems.

I have a wonderful wife (Victoria) who is very supportive of me. We are both active members of our church. I love preaching the gospel and going to different churches to tell my story, of how one day I was supposed to die and God gave me a second chance.

CPSIA information can be obtained
at www.ICGtesting.com
Printed in the USA
FSHW021157070319
56059FS

9 781532 388941